Evaluating Methods to Estimate the Effect of State Laws on Firearm Deaths

A Simulation Study

Terry L. Schell, Beth Ann Griffin, Andrew R. Morral

A PART OF THE RAND

INITIATIVE

For more information on this publication, visit www.rand.org/t/RR2685

Library of Congress Cataloging-in-Publication Data is available for this publication.
ISBN: 978-1-9774-0155-7

Published by the RAND Corporation, Santa Monica, Calif.
© Copyright 2018 RAND Corporation
RAND® is a registered trademark.

www.rand.org

Preface

The RAND Corporation launched its Gun Policy in America initiative in January 2016 with the goal of creating objective, factual resources for policymakers and the public on the effects of gun laws. As a part of this project, RAND conducted a systematic literature review and evaluation of scientific studies on the effects of 14 classes of policies on eight outcomes related to gun ownership, including outcomes of concern to those who favor policies that limit access to and use of firearms and those who favor laws that expand such access and use (detailed in the report *The Science of Gun Policy: A Critical Synthesis of Research Evidence on the Effects of Gun Policies in the United States*). The results of this study suggested that relatively little consistent and persuasive evidence could be found describing the effects of most gun policies. In part, this appeared to result from the sensitivity of such estimates to statistical modeling choices made by investigators. Of course, different statistical models imply different assumptions about the data, some of which may be right, but some of which must be wrong if different approaches lead to different inferences about the effects of laws.

This report systematically investigates the performance of a wide range of statistical models commonly used in the gun policy literature to estimate the effects of gun policies on firearm deaths at the state level. The goal of this study is to identify the most appropriate statistical modeling and analysis methods for producing these estimates, which should provide useful information in evaluating whether estimates from prior research should be considered to be accurate or inaccurate.

This report should be of interest to researchers familiar with statistical methods for estimating causal effects in longitudinal time series data, those who are trying to understand the effects of gun policies as revealed in the existing literature, or those who are planning new studies that use statistical models to investigate these effects.

RAND Ventures

The RAND Corporation is a research organization that develops solutions to public policy challenges to help make communities throughout the world safer and more secure, healthier, and more prosperous. RAND is nonprofit, nonpartisan, and committed to the public interest.

RAND Ventures is a vehicle for investing in such policy solutions. Philanthropic contributions support our ability to take the long view, tackle tough and often-controversial topics, and share our findings in innovative and compelling ways. RAND's research findings and recommendations are based on data and evidence and therefore do not necessarily reflect the policy preferences or interests of its clients, donors, or supporters.

Funding for this venture was provided by gifts from RAND supporters and income from operations. This report received additional support through a grant from the Laura and John Arnold Foundation.

Contents

Figure and Tables

Figure

Tables

Summary

There is a growing scientific literature investigating the effects of gun policies on firearm deaths. Unfortunately, reviewers of this literature have frequently concluded that strong claims about the effects of most gun laws cannot be made because estimates of their effects appear to be especially sensitive to statistical modeling choices made by investigators (see, for example, Hahn et al., 2005; National Research Council, 2004; RAND Corporation, 2018). Different modeling choices typically imply different assumptions about the data. However, no study to date has comprehensively examined which assumptions might be most appropriate for the type of data being examined in gun policy research. In this report, we describe how we used statistical simulations to identify the most appropriate model for estimating the causal effects of laws or policies on state-level total firearm deaths between 1979 and 2014.

Our goal with this evaluation was to establish whether some commonly used statistical models have better statistical performance than others on four primary criteria: (1) type 1 error rates (the rate of statistically significant effect estimates when the law actually has no effect), (2) statistical power (the rate of correct rejections of the null hypothesis when the law has a true effect), (3) directional bias (bias that results in estimates of a law's effects that are, on average, offset from the true value by either a consistently positive or a consistently negative value), and (4) magnitude bias (bias that results in effect estimates that are too close to zero or too extreme [i.e., the absolute value of the estimates is consistently too small or, conversely, consistently too large]).

These simulations used actual state-level data on firearm deaths and other state-specific demographic and economic variables between 1979 and 2014. In each simulation, a subset of states was randomly selected to be counted as having "implemented" an unspecified gun law during the period. The date of implementation of the law was chosen at random for each randomly selected state. Once the simulated "law" was implemented, it remained in effect for the duration of the available data. Because these "laws" occurred at random, they had no true association with state firearm deaths. In other simulations, we not only randomly assigned laws but also modified the firearm death rates in the states with the law so that the law was associated with a true treatment effect. That is, each state with the law had its firearm death rates adjusted either up or down in each year the law was in effect. Taken together, therefore, the relationship between the simulated laws and total firearm deaths was varied across three *effect conditions*: The simulated laws could have a true negative effect, no effect, or a true positive effect on firearm deaths.

In addition to varying the effect of the simulated law, we also varied how many states implemented it (three, 15, or 35 states) and how long it took for the law to take full effect (instant or five-year phase-in). In total, therefore, there were 18 simulation conditions (three law *effect conditions* by three law *prevalence conditions* by two *phase-in conditions*). Five thousand simulated data sets were created for each of these 18 conditions, and models were evaluated based on their average performance across simulations within a condition.

The statistical models (and methods for adjusting model standard errors [SEs]) we examined were diverse, representing most of the models commonly described in empirical studies of the effects of gun laws. Specifically, we examined models that incorporated various combinations of the following features:

- the model link function (linear and log-link)
- the use of a logarithmic transformation of the outcome variable (firearm death rate)
- the use of population weights
- the inclusion of autoregressive effects

- the type of coding used for the law's effect: effect versus change coding (see "Inclusion of Autoregressive Effects" section in Chapter Two)
- the inclusion of state-fixed or random effects
- the inclusion of state-specific linear trends
- the use of general estimating equations
- the use of SE adjustments for clustering by state
- the use of robustness adjustments to the SE.

The results of these simulations reveal that many commonly used modeling approaches in gun policy research have quite poor type 1 error rates. Indeed, several models have type 1 error rates ten times greater than the nominal $\alpha = 0.05$ that was intended. In general, Huber and cluster adjustments often do not fix these problems and sometimes make them worse. The models also had surprisingly low statistical power to detect an effect-sized equivalent to a change of 1,000 deaths per year if a law were implemented nationally. Most models could correctly reject the null hypothesis only about 10 percent of the time with this true effect. With power this low, a large fraction of effects that are statistically significant will be found to be in the opposite direction as the true effect, and all will greatly exaggerate the magnitude of the true effect.

One model was identified as having the best performance across all assessed criteria. This model is a negative binomial model of firearm deaths that includes time-fixed effects, an autoregressive lag, and change coding for the law effect. The preferred specification includes no state-fixed effects or SE adjustment.

In addition to demonstrating the best performance with respect to statistical inference and generally low bias in the effect estimates, the preferred model was also found to offer the best protection against confounds because of omitted covariates and against artifacts caused by regression to the mean. It also was better at ensuring that the causal variable—enactment of the law—preceded the measured change in firearm death rates.

Although one statistical approach performed better in our simulations, all models had relatively low power to detect a meaningfully large effect size. For this reason, we recommend that researchers consider using Bayesian statistical methods when estimating the effect of state laws on firearm death rates. Rather than attempting to produce a dichotomous classification of each effect as either statistically significant or not, Bayesian methods describe the range of possible true effects that are consistent with the available data (given the model and the researcher-specified priors). Given the lack of power to conduct traditional significant testing, policymakers will be well served to understand the range of possible effects associated with a given policy and where the weight of current evidence lies.

Acknowledgments

We wish to acknowledge the work of one of our RAND colleagues, Samantha Cherney, who led development of the RAND State Firearm Law database that was used in the analyses reported here. In addition, we gratefully acknowledge the helpful reviews of earlier drafts of this report provided by Edward Kennedy of Carnegie Mellon University and Claude Setodji at the RAND Corporation.

Abbreviations

BLS	Bureau of Labor Statistics
CDC	Centers for Disease Control and Prevention
GEE	general estimating equation
SE	standard error

CHAPTER ONE

Introduction

There is a growing literature that attempts to empirically estimate the causal effects of firearm policies across a range of crime and health outcomes. Typically, these studies exploit the natural experiments offered when U.S. states adopt similar laws but in different years. Using such statistical approaches as difference-in-differences models, these studies attempt to identify the effects of such laws on state-level measurements of suicides, homicides, or other crime outcomes. In a recent review of this literature, researchers at the RAND Corporation identified 63 studies that examined the effects of 13 types of gun policies. Surprisingly, this review concluded that these studies do not yet support strong conclusions about the effects of most gun policies.

One of the barriers to drawing conclusions from the existing gun policy literature is that estimated effects depend to a remarkable extent on the specific statistical methods they use (see also National Research Council, 2004; Durlauf, Navarro, and Rivers, 2016). Frequently, studies using the same data sources but different statistical methods produce different and even contradictory conclusions about the effects of a given law.

When many studies produce a wide range of effect estimates, gun policy advocates often highlight those findings that are most consistent with their policy objectives, and the wider public and policymakers may become confused about what the true effect of such gun policies might be. In these situations, it is not uncommon to find meta-analyses designed to establish the average observed effect across studies. These techniques generally assume that separate effect estimates

1

are derived from independent data sources. In the gun policy literature, however, studies are frequently not independent observations on different data sources. The studies producing different estimates often use the same data set or data sets that are subsets of one another. In such a case, the variation in estimated effects are not due to random variation across independent samples but are due to studies making different statistical assumptions. When these studies arrive at inconsistent conclusions about the effects of gun laws, some of the differences result from reliance on assumptions that are inappropriate for the data. The estimates from studies making less-appropriate assumptions should be discarded—not averaged together—with the other estimates on the same general data.

Another common practice in the literature is for researchers to conduct the impact analysis many different ways, producing as many as 100 different estimates of the causal effects of the policy, each making slightly different assumptions or estimating effects on different subsamples. These estimates often vary in magnitude over a wide range, as well as in their level of statistical significance. Researchers then use their subjective judgment to select which model or models to emphasize in their conclusions. This creates substantial hazards for drawing correct inferences, as the estimated effects are subject to many "researcher degrees of freedom" (Simmons, Nelson, and Simonsohn, 2011)—that is, statistical inferences may be shaped by the many subjective modeling choices made by the analyst, as well as by the high risk of an incorrect rejection of the null hypothesis due to multiple testing.

Instead of averaging effect estimates across multiple statistical methods or subjectively selecting a preferred model after seeing the results of dozens of candidate models, it is better to select the statistical method that is most appropriate to the specific data being analyzed andestimate the effect using only that method. We demonstrate here a principled approach to selecting the most-appropriate modeling assumptions and statistical methods for a given set of data. This approach evaluated the performance of different statistical models on real, or minimally altered, data where the effects of gun laws have been simulated. Therefore, this approach allowed for the selection of methods that should be preferred over less-appropriate methods.

We used statistical simulations to identify the most appropriate model for analyzing how laws contribute to state-level variation in total firearm deaths. These simulations used actual state-level data on firearm deaths and other state-specific demographic and economic variables between 1979 and 2014. In each simulation, a randomly selected subset of states was treated as though each introduced a new (but unspecified) gun law on a randomly selected date. Because these "laws" occurred at random, they had no true association with state firearm deaths. In other simulations, we not only randomly assigned laws to states but also slightly modified the firearm death rates in the states with the law so that the law was associated with a true treatment effect of known size. That is, each state with the law had its firearm death rate adjusted either up or down in each year the law was in effect. Taken together, therefore, the relationship between the simulated laws and total firearm deaths was varied across three effect conditions: The simulated laws could have a true negative effect, a null effect (no effect), or a true positive effect.

We then used a wide range of statistical methods to estimate the causal effect of these simulated policies on firearm deaths when the policies do and do not have a true effect. This allows us to identify those statistical models that perform best on four main criteria: (1) type 1 error rates (the rate of statistically significant effect estimates when the law actually has no effect), (2) statistical power (the rate of correct rejections of the null hypothesis when the law has a true effect), (3) directional bias (bias in the effect estimates that results in estimates that are, on average, offset from the true value by either a consistently positive or a consistently negative value), and (4) magnitude bias (bias in the estimates that results in their being too close to zero or too extreme [i.e., the absolute value of the estimates is consistently too small or, conversely, consistently too large]).

We selected firearm deaths as the outcome to simulate in this study, as opposed to other possible crime or societal outcomes, for three reasons: First, there is a clear basis for the hypothesis that state-level firearm policies affect firearm deaths because that is often the explicit goal of the legislation. By focusing narrowly on outcomes for which we have strong hypotheses, we avoid exploratory analyses that could bias statistical inference. Second, firearm homicides and suicides are important societal outcomes. Even small effects of regulations on these deaths are more important to crafting good public policy than nominally larger effects on less weighty outcomes. In our recent survey of gun policy experts, the experts' overall evaluation of specific gun regulations was primarily associated with their beliefs about the policy's effect on firearm homicides and other firearm fatalities (RAND Corporation, 2018). This finding was true for experts drawn from the gun rights community, the gun control community, and academic researchers. Experts from each group favored policies they believe will reduce firearm homicides and suicides. For this reason, we believe empirical research focused narrowly on the effect of policy on deaths has the most potential for improving firearm policies.

Finally, we focused on firearm deaths because they are well measured relative to other outcomes of gun policy. Virtually all deaths caused by firearms are logged into a national database using a common classification scheme, regardless of jurisdiction. In contrast, most other types of outcomes used to evaluate gun policy are subject to a range of measurement biases that vary across states and over time. These may substantially influence the modeled effects of state-level policies. For example, some research focuses on the effect of gun policy on crime outcomes, such as burglary. However, the number of burglaries for a given jurisdiction in a given year within the Uniform Crime Reports is influenced by variation across jurisdictions in the percentage of burglaries that are reported to police, as well as substantial variation across jurisdictions and over time in the completeness of the records voluntarily submitted to the Federal Bureau of Investigation.

CHAPTER TWO

Methods

The goal of the study was to assess the performance of a wide range of statistical models for estimating the effect of a state law on firearm death rates using four criteria: (1) the type 1 error rates, (2) correct rejection rates (statistical power) for statistical inferences, (3) directional bias, and (4) magnitude bias in the effect estimates themselves. We used each candidate model to estimate the effects of laws in 5,000 simulated data sets in which the laws' effects are known. Using state-level data from 1981 to 2009, these simulated data sets were constructed by randomly selecting a subset of states to "implement" the unspecified law in a year selected at random during the time period. Although the laws were simulated, outcome data (firearm deaths) and state demographic and economic characteristics used as model covariates were based on the actual state-year time-series data. The relationship between the simulated laws and total firearm deaths was varied across three effect conditions: The simulated laws could have a true negative effect, no effect, or a true positive effect on firearm deaths.

In addition to varying the true effect of the law, we also varied how many states implemented it (three, 15, or 35 states) and how long it took for the law's full effect to phase in (instantaneously or five years). In total, there were 18 simulation conditions (three law *effect conditions* by three law *prevalence conditions* by two *phase-in conditions*). Five thousand simulated data sets were created for each of these 18 conditions, and models were evaluated based on their average performance across simulations within each condition.

We examined diverse statistical models (and methods for adjusting model standard errors [SEs]), representing most of the models commonly described in empirical studies of the effects of gun laws. Specifically, we examined models that incorporated various combinations of the following features:

- the model link function (linear and log link)
- the use of a logarithmic transformation of the outcome variable
- the use of population weights
- the inclusion of autoregressive effects
- the type of coding used for the law effect
- the inclusion of state-fixed or random effects
- the inclusion of state-specific linear trends
- the use of general estimating equations (GEEs)
- the use of SE adjustments for clustering by state
- the use of robustness adjustments to the SE.

Criteria for Assessing Performance of Statistical Models

The simulation study was designed to identify the statistical model that was most appropriate for estimating the effect of a given state-level policy on firearm deaths. Specifically, we assessed the following four model performance criteria (ordered to represent our view of their importance in guiding the selection of appropriate methods):

- *Type 1 error rate.* When the null hypothesis is true, the model of choice should reject the null 5 percent of the time if tested with an $\alpha = 0.05$ level of significance. In other words, the estimated SE of the law's effect should accurately reflect the actual uncertainty in the estimated effect.
- *Correct rejection rate of the null (statistical power).* When the null hypothesis is false (e.g., there is a true effect of a law) and tested with a true type 1 error rate of 5 percent, models are preferred that have a higher probability of rejecting the null hypoth-

esis in the correct direction. This represents the statistical power or efficiency of the model to measure the effect.

- *Directional bias.* The estimated effect for a good model should not be biased toward finding either positive or negative effects. This implies, for example, that if one policy increased firearm deaths and another policy decreased deaths by the same amount, the two effects estimated within the same type of model should average to zero over a large number of simulations rather than show bias in the direction of the positive or negative estimates.
- *Magnitude bias.* When the null hypothesis is false, the estimated effect size should not be biased either toward zero or away from zero. That is to say, the estimated effect should, on average, be on the proper scale, rather than being shrunk toward zero or exaggerated in magnitude.

In addition to these four primary criteria that are directly assessed through the simulations, we also investigated four additional model-selection criteria. These desirable model characteristics included (1) model estimates that were more robust with respect to omitted covariates, (2) model estimates that were less subject to bias caused by regression to the mean, (3) models that required temporal precedence (i.e., that the law must be implemented prior to the shift in death rates in order for that shift to produce an estimated causal effect), and (4) models that did not require empirical corrections to the SEs (e.g., cluster adjustments) to compensate for mis-specified likelihood functions. While the use of such corrections is sometimes necessary, using them typically prevents the use of likelihood ratio tests, makes most model fit indices inaccurate, and may indicate broader problems with the model.

Design of the Simulation

The simulation used actual state-level, annual firearm death rates from 1979 to 2014 (excluding the District of Columbia), as well as covariates that measure key features of each state in each year. This 36-year period was chosen because most of the gun policies evaluated in the literature we reviewed were implemented since 1980, and the period corresponded to the period over which this outcome and the covariates are well measured. Annual state death rates were drawn from the Center for Disease Control and Prevention's (CDC's) WONDER online data analysis tool (CDC, 2018). When simulating laws with either positive or negative effects, the CDC data have been modified to incorporate a true effect for each state in each year that the randomly introduced law was in effect.

The true variation in firearm death rates over time is shown in Figure 1.1 for all 50 states, with a bold line representing the national average. The overall data series shows dramatic differences in firearm

Figure 2.1
Total Firearm Death Rate, by Year and State

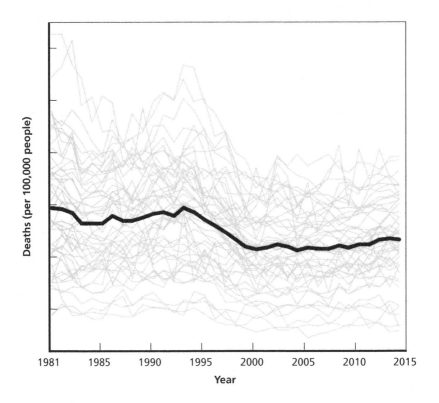

death rates across states, more pronounced in the earlier years of the data series. It also shows a general decline in the rates over the period, particularly during the 1990s. Finally, the state trend lines differ substantially in the extent to which they display large year-over-year variation in the death rates, with some states having rates that varied by 15 deaths per 100,000 people through the period, while the death rate in other states varied by less than two deaths per 100,000 people. Although not represented in the figure, the states that show larger year-to-year variability in their rates tend to be those with smaller populations.

The random variation across simulation trials was introduced by randomly selecting a specific number of states to "implement" a simulated law and then randomly generating an implementation date for each of those states. The simulated law remained in effect for the remainder of the time period.

Law Effect Conditions

Data sets simulated in the null or no effect conditions had "laws" randomly assigned to states. Because these laws occurred at random, they had no true association with state firearm deaths. Under these conditions, a properly calibrated model should reject the null hypothesis that these laws had no effect approximately 5 percent of the time using $\alpha = 0.05$. We recorded the actual proportion of these rejections for each model to assess the first criterion—their *type 1 error rates* (or false positive rates). Better-calibrated models will have type 1 error rates closer to 5 percent.

In addition to assessing rates of type 1 error, the results under the null hypothesis also provided us with an SE correction factor for each model being evaluated. This is computed by analyzing the empirical distribution (over the replications) of the effect estimate to identify a critical value such that only 5 percent of the estimates in the simulation were more extreme. The ratio of the simulated critical value to the critical value produced by the modeled SE and test statistic serves as the correction factor. Thus, the SE correction factor represents the value that, when multiplied by the modeled SE, gives a corrected SE that achieves a 5-percent type 1 error rate in the simulation under the null hypothesis. We used this correction factor later when evaluating each model's probability of correctly rejecting the null hypothesis when the alternative hypothesis is true.

We used data sets simulated under the positive and negative law effect conditions to assess the other three primary performance criteria: correct rejection rates, directional bias, and magnitude bias. To generate these simulated data sets, we took the same sample of simulated laws that were used to test performance under the null hypothesis but altered the outcome variable to incorporate a true causal effect for each state and year when the law was in effect. For example, we could modify the firearm death data so that each simulated law creates a 10-percent decrease in risk of firearm death. This could be done by first determining the effect size in each year by multiplying the actual firearm deaths in a given state-year by 0.10 times the variable indicating the simulated law's presence in that state-year (with the "law" variable coded such that zero indicates no law in that state-year and one indicates a year in which the law was fully implemented), then subtracting that effect from the actual number of deaths recorded for each state and year. Similarly, we could create a true 10-percent increase in deaths by adding the same effect size to the actual number of deaths. Once the data were modified to create a real relationship between the simulated laws and firearm deaths, each model was run 5,000 times per condition to determine how well it could recover that true effect. Each model was tested using two alternative hypotheses, one in which the simulated law increased firearm deaths and one in which it decreased firearm deaths by the same amount.

All of our simulations under alternative hypotheses (i.e., in the conditions with positive or negative law effects) were conducted using an effect size that would result in a national change in firearm deaths of 1,000 per year in an average year if the law were implemented in all 50 states relative to a scenario in which it was not implemented in any state. Our view is that policymaker decisions should be influenced by knowledge that a given law could either cause or prevent 1,000 deaths nationally in each year. Thus, it would be problematic for a statistical model to have inadequate power to assess a true effect of this size when using all available data. An increase or decrease of 1,000 firearm deaths represents about a 3-percent change over the average deaths per year. This is a relatively small effect expressed as a percentage, although it is large in a practical sense (1,000 is a lot of lives to save or lose each year) and probably represents a fairly optimistic goal for an effective gun policy. For example, a policy that could eliminate all mass shootings in the country would save fewer than 1,000 people per year but would be considered a successful and important policy. Similarly, a policy that resulted in the doubling of accidental firearm deaths would be one that had an effect smaller than 1,000 deaths per year.

This effect size was also seen as large enough to be important within a RAND survey of gun policy experts drawn from both the gun control and gun rights communities (Morral, Schell, and Tankard, 2018). Specifically, we surveyed policy experts on their favorability toward 15 specific gun policies, as well as their beliefs about the expected effects of these policies. We found that experts strongly favored policies when they believed their effects size was large enough to reduce either suicides or homicides by 1,000 incidents nationally (i.e., a 3-percent shift in both homicides and suicides) and strongly opposed policies that they believed would increase deaths by a similar amount. This finding was true both for those experts who generally wanted stricter gun regulations and those who wanted to reduce gun regulations (although these two types of experts disagreed on which policies would produce those changes).

We tailored the effect size of 1,000 deaths to the specific link function used in the model. In a linear model predicting death rates, we added to or subtracted 0.3831 per 100,000 people from the actual death rate in any year in which the simulated law was fully in effect. This effect would not produce a change of exactly 1,000 deaths in each year but would result in an average effect of 1,000 deaths over the years of data being analyzed. In contrast, models using a log link assumed that the true effect was multiplicative rather than additive. When creating data under the alternative hypothesis for use in testing these models, we multiplied the actual number of firearm deaths by a factor of either $\exp(0.0301) = 1.0305$ or $\exp(-0.0301) = 0.9704$ for those state-years in which the simulated law was in full effect ($\exp$ = exponentiation). This effect size also resulted in an average change of 1,000 deaths per year across the years in the data set, although the precise effect varied by year. Thus, each type of model had the same average effect size within the sample, although these effects were built into the simulation data in different ways so that they were consistent with the assumptions of each type of model.

For all of the models we investigated, this estimated treatment effect was taken from a single-model parameter. For example, a true positive causal effect for a linear model was built into the data by adding the quantity b^*x to the observed firearm death rate for each state in each year, where b is the effect size expressed as deaths per 100,000 people, and x is the randomly generated indicator of the implementation status of the law in each state and year. We then estimated a linear model in which we used the vector of x as a predictor and assessed how well the model recovered the true coefficient, b. The same procedure was used for log-link models, except that b was scaled as the log risk ratio rather than the difference in death rates.

The alternative hypothesis simulations for a given model provide 5,000 effect estimates with a true positive effect and 5,000 estimates with a true negative effect. From these, we can compute the other three criteria used for model selection. We defined the rate of correct rejections for each model as the proportion of estimates that were both statistically significant and in the same direction as the true effect. When conducting this significance test, we used the corrected SEs computed in the simulations under the null hypothesis. This way, rates of correct rejections could be compared across models that have the exact same type 1 error rate. Without applying the SE correction factor, models that underestimate the true error in their estimates would appear to have excellent statistical power, even though the actual sampling variability in their estimates may be quite high, in which case the model may not actually be sensitive to detecting a true effect.

For many of the models we tested, there were multiple ways commonly used to compute SEs (e.g., with and without a cluster adjustment, with and without a Huber correction). We investigated these methods in the simulation. For the purpose of investigating the *correct rejection rate* for a given model, we adopted the method of computing the SE that had the SE correction factor closest to one in the simulations under the null hypothesis. For example, if clustering-adjusted SEs resulted in a type 1 error rate closer to 5 percent in the simulations under the null for a given model, then, when investigating the correct rejection rate for that model, we applied that clustering adjustment (as well as the corresponding SE correction factor measured in the simulation) when conducting significance tests. When presenting the correct rejection rate for any model, we average the rate across the positive and negative effect simulations.

To assess *directional bias* in the estimated causal effects of the simulated laws, we compared a model's estimates when there was a true positive effect to when there was a true negative effect. Because these two effects were built into the data as equal in magnitude but in opposite directions, the average of the effects across the 10,000 simulations should be zero. In other words, the model estimates should not be biased toward finding that the simulated laws increase firearm deaths or decrease them. Because the actual time series has substantial trends over time, it is possible that some methods for estimating the causal effect will be biased toward yielding either positive or negative values. Such a bias could be a substantial threat to the validity of statistical inferences drawn from the model.

Magnitude bias assesses the tendency of the estimated effects of a given model to fall closer to zero or further from zero than the true effect. This is computed by taking the average of the coefficients across the positive and negative effect simulations, after multiplying the coefficients from the negative effect simulations by negative one; this gives the average effect magnitude. We get magnitude bias by subtracting that value from the true effect size. Magnitude bias is not necessarily a threat to the validity of statistical inferences (i.e., a significant effect indicating an increase in deaths is still likely to indicate a true increase in deaths), but it does make it difficult to interpret the effects. Essentially, the model coefficients are not expressed in the expected units. For example, with a model that shows a magnitude bias of +0.1 with a true effect size of 0.30, the model typically gives estimates of +0.4 or −0.4 for the positive and negative effects, respectively, exaggerating the true effect size.

To facilitate comparisons across models with different link functions, all of the estimated effects have been converted into linear effects prior to assessing bias. Specifically, the effects are expressed in terms of the change in the total number of firearm deaths if the law had been implemented and fully phased in across the nation in an average year. The original effect for linear models is expressed as a change in the annual firearm death rate; it was converted to a count of deaths by multiplying that change in death rate by the full population of the United States in an average year over the period. The original effect for log-link models is expressed as a log-relative risk; it was converted to a count of deaths by exponentiating the log-relative risk and multiplying it by the number of firearm deaths in the nation in an average year. Regardless of the link function, the true, simulated effect size for both types of models corresponded to +1,000 deaths or −1,000 deaths for the positive and negative effect conditions, respectively. If the model produced an average effect estimate of +1,000 across the 5,000 simulated laws in the positive condition, and −1,000 in the negative condition, it showed no *directional* bias or *magnitude* bias. On the other hand, if the model averaged +1,100 in the positive condition and −900 in the negative, it showed a *directional* bias of +100 and zero *magnitude* bias. Finally, a model that averaged effects of +1,100 in the positive condition and −1,100 in the negative, showed no *directional* bias but a *magnitude* bias of +100.

Law Prevalence and Phase-in Conditions

We systematically varied the characteristics of the simulated laws to better cover the range of real laws that we wished to investigate (three different states implementing the law by two different phase-in periods). The first characteristic that we varied was the number of states that were randomly selected to have implemented the law. This was designed to range from a relatively large number of states (35), which is typical for the most popular state firearm policies, down to three states. While many of the models could be estimated on a single state, our view is that it is difficult to interpret the causal effect of the law because of multiple confounding historical events in the state that were concurrent with the law (Standish, Cook, and Campbell, 2002). Choosing three to be the minimum number of states to implement a law reflects our view that, at a minimum, this number of observations is necessary to reasonably begin to identify a possible causal effect. In addition to simulating three and 35 state conditions, we also simulated a 15-state condition between those two.

We also investigated two phase-in periods for the law's effects. Laws could have an instantaneous effect, implemented as a simple step function that has a value of zero when the law is not in effect and a value of one when the law is fully in effect. Alternatively, the law's effect could phase in over time. We simulated a law whose effect phases in linearly over a five-year period. This was implemented as a linear spline with values starting at zero and reaching an asymptote at one—five years after the law's implementation. Within the simulation, the assumed phase-in period used in the model being estimated was always the same one that was used to create the effect within the simulated data. True instant effects were fit with models assuming the effect would be instant; true five-year phase-in effects were fit assuming a five-year phase-in. In practical applications, the true phase-in period will not be known. Because of this, the simulations likely overestimated the statistical power that would be achieved in practice.

In creating each randomly generated "law," we first selected a random set of states to implement the law (three, 15, or 35 states), then randomly selected an implementation date for those states. Specifically, an implementation month was randomly selected with all months between January 1981 and December 2009 having an equal probability of selection. We did not simulate implementation dates in the first two years or the last five years of the data series. This was done under the assumption that researchers would generally avoid investigating causal effects if they did not have outcome data for the implementing states over a reasonable period of time both before and after implementation (particularly if assuming a five-year phase-in period). Thus, the current simulation will overestimate power for analyses in which the law in question sometimes falls at the very end or very beginning of the data series.

The modeled outcome was the rate of firearm deaths over a calendar year; however, the simulated implementation dates may occur any time during a calendar year, meaning the full effect of the first year of a law may be split across calendar years. The statistical modes used in the simulation account for this misalignment by modifying the effect coding. Specifically, the effect coding in a given calendar year was calculated as the average monthly causal effect over that year. Thus, even in the instantaneous effect simulations, the effect coding took on fractional values. For example, a law that had an instantaneous effect and was implemented on July 1, 2000, would be coded as a 0.0 in 1999, a 0.5 in 2000 (to reflect the full effect of the law, but applied to half of a year), and a 1.0 in 2001, the first full year of the law's effect. Because of this, the effect of a law that had an instant effect at the time it was implemented often took two years to fully appear in the annual death data; an effect that phases in over five years would typically takes six years to fully influence the annual death data. (An example is provided later in Chapter Two, when we discuss variations in effect coding.)

Statistical Models Investigated

Features Common to All Models

Two model features were kept constant across all of the models in the simulations. The first feature was that all models included fixed effects for each year of the data series, which effectively controls for national trends in firearm death rates. The second feature was that all models included the same set of covariates.

The state characteristics that were included as covariates were intended to be relatively comprehensive. The set included most characteristics that have been found by other researchers to be associated with firearm deaths, as well as variables that are commonly used when analyzing state-level differences in health or crime. These variables were all taken from publicly available sources and constitute descriptive statistics for each state for each year in the studied period. The 36 original variables are shown in Table 2.1.

The three firearm-related variables lagged in time such that the values predicting a given year's firearm death rate were taken from the prior year for that state. This was done because such factors are plau-

Table 2.1
State Characteristics Used in the Modeling

Type (and Variable)	Source
Age distribution (percentages)	U.S. Census Bureau (undated)
Younger than 15	
15–29	
30–44	
45–60	
60–75	
Older than 75	
Race or ethnicity (percentages)	U.S. Census Bureau (undated)
White	
African American	
Asian/Pacific Islander	
American Indian/Alaska Native	
Hispanic	U.S. Census Bureau (undated)
Relationship status (percentages)	IPUMS CPS (undated)
Married/widowed	
Divorced	
Never married	
Highest education (percentages)	IPUMS CPS (undated)
Without high school diploma	
High school diploma	
Four-year degree	
Graduate degree	
Other demographics	
Total population size	CDC WONDER (CDC, 2018)
Gender ratio	U.S. Census Bureau (undated)
Percentage of children in single-parent household	IPUMS CPS (undated)
Percentage foreign born	IPUMS CPS (undated)
Percentage military veterans	IPUMS CPS (undated)
Percentage urban households	IPUMS CPS (undated)
Percentage > 25 years old, black, and urban	IPUMS CPS (undated)
Percentage > 25 years old, Hispanic, and urban	IPUMS CPS (undated)

Table 2.1—Continued

Type (and Variable)	Source
Socioeconomic conditions	
Percentage of population in the workforce	U.S. Department of Labor, Bureau of Labor Statistics (BLS) (undated)
Percentage unemployed (official unemployment rate, or *U3*)	U.S. Department of Labor, BLS (undated)
Average income (inflation adjusted)	Bureau of Economic Analysis (2016)
Poverty rate	U.S. Census Bureau (2018)
Alcohol consumption per capita	National Institute on Alcohol Abuse and Alcoholism (2016)
Incarcerated persons per capita	Bureau of Justice Statistics (undated)
Police officers per capita	U.S. Department of Justice, Federal Bureau of Investigation (2016)
Firearm-related measures[a]	
Proportion of firearm deaths that are suicide	CDC WONDER (CDC, 2018)
Rate of nonfirearm suicides	CDC WONDER (CDC, 2018)
Percentage receiving hunting license	U.S. Fish and Wildlife Service (2018)

[a] These covariates are plausibly the effects of gun control policies, as well as possible confounds for estimating the policy's effects. For this reason, they are lagged one year; they predict firearm deaths in the subsequent year rather than in the year they are measured.

sibly influenced by the firearm regulations whose effects we will ultimately be estimating; that is, they are endogenous to the policies in question. By lagging these variables, we decrease the risk of accidently controlling for the causal effect that we are attempting to measure when applying the model to real-world laws.

Prior to analysis, a few of these state characteristics were cleaned or transformed to mitigate undesirable properties. Specifically, in a few cases in which values were missing for a given state-year, we imputed values using linear interpolation between the prior-year and subsequent-year values for that state. For a few predictors with extreme outliers, we also applied modest transformations to limit the influence of outlier values. Specifically, we applied the minimal power transformation (e.g., square root) that ensured all values were within five standard deviations of the mean.

Finally, we conducted additional transformations of the state characteristics to address the high degree of collinearity among some of these variables. Specifically, we used dimension-reduction techniques to capture most of the information contained in the full list of correlated variables with a smaller number of orthogonal variables. To do this, we (1) removed from each covariate the variance that is collinear with the year fixed effects that will be included in all of the models and (2) used principal components analysis to linearly transform the matrix of standardized covariates into an ordered set of orthogonal variables (or principal components). The models used the first 17 of these principal components, which were selected because those variables could explain more than 95 percent of the variance in the full matrix of state characteristics. Using this transformed matrix of covariates makes more efficient use of the available data; virtually all of the information contained in the original 36 state characteristics can be captured using only 17 model parameters. Using the smaller set of orthogonal predictors also speeds maximum likelihood estimation of the models and may prevent some methodological artifacts that can occur when modeling highly collinear predictors. The downside of using the transformed covariates is that the modeled effects of individual covariates are not substantively interpretable. As our focus in these simulations is on understanding the qualities of different model types and their effect estimates, we had no need for interpreting the covariates.

Range of Models Evaluated

Researchers analyzing longitudinal data use a range of statistical models and different methods of estimating SEs, depending on the type of data being analyzed and various disciplinary traditions. In the next subsections, we outline the broad differences in statistical methods that we investigated within our simulation study. Appendix A provides formal definitions of each of the models investigated. The R code used to implement each model is included in the online technical appendix.

Model Link and Likelihood Function

Within this literature, there are three broad classes of models that are typically used: models with a linear link function, a log-link function, or a linear link function with a log-transformed outcome value. Linear models of rate outcomes are fairly common in this field (see, for example, Gius, 2014, 2015a, 2015b; Webster, Crifasi, and

Vernick, 2014; Raissian, 2016). For example, these models might express the firearm death rate (e.g., deaths per 100,000 people) for each state in each year as a linear combination of predictors and normally distributed error that is independent across observations.

One popular alternative to a linear model is a log-link model, typically Poisson (see, for example, Cheng and Hoekstra, 2013; Crifasi et al., 2015; Cummings et al., 1997; DeSimone, Markowitz, and Xu, 2013; Gius, 2015c; Grambsch, 2008; Hepburn et al., 2006; Kalesan et al., 2016; Lott, 2003; Rosengart et al., 2005; Zeoli and Webster, 2010) or negative binomial (see, for example, Ludwig and Cook, 2000; Roberts, 2009; Sen and Panjamapirom, 2012; Vigdor and Mercy, 2006; Webster and Starnes, 2000; Webster et al., 2004). These models predict the numeric count of the outcomes (firearm deaths) within a state in a given year; however, they include the logarithm of state population size as an offset. This results in a model that is effectively predicting the firearm death rate, and exponentiated model coefficients are interpreted as incident risk ratios (e.g., a 1.10 effect is interpreted as a 10-percent increase in the firearm death rate). These models make several different assumptions than the linear model; for example, log-link models assume that the outcome is always positive, the error in the estimates is not symmetrically distributed, and the error in the death rate is not identical across observations made on different-sized populations. Specifically, these models assume that random variability in the measured death rate is larger for states with low populations and smaller for more-populous states. We evaluated the negative binomial, Poisson, and quasi-Poisson models in our simulation, but the negative binomial model always outperformed the other two. Thus, to simplify presentation, we present the results only for the negative binomial models in this report.

We also investigated log-linear (or log-normal) models, which are commonly used in the gun policy literature (e.g., Aneja, Donohue, and Zhang, 2014; Cheng and Hoekstra, 2013; Kendall and Tamura, 2010; Kovandzic, Marvell, and Vieraitis, 2005; La Valle, 2013; La Valle and Glover, 2012; Lott, 2010; Lott and Mustard, 1997; Martin and Legault, 2005). These are linear models conducted on the natural logarithm of the outcome rather than the outcome in its natural units. These models have some of the features of a log-link model: Their exponentiated model coefficients are interpreted as incident risk ratios, the assumed error in the death rate is not symmetrical, and the model assumes that the death rate cannot be negative. Unlike the log-link model, however, error variability is assumed to be constant across states of different populations. These models are generally limited to data in which there are no observations with an outcome value of exactly zero (the log of zero is undefined); however, this is not a limitation when looking at firearm death rates for specific state-year, as all states had at least one such death in each year.

As discussed earlier, when evaluating a log-link or log-linear model, we built simulated data sets in which the true effect was built into the data as a factor multiplied by the true death rate. When evaluating the linear models, we built in true effects by adding a constant to the death rate. While both ways of creating the effects are equivalent in magnitude in an average year (increasing or decreasing the deaths by 1,000 if applied nationally), different methods are used so that the form of the causal effect fits the assumptions of the underlying model being assessed.

Controlling for Differences Across States

Another factor we varied across models is how, or whether, they attempt to control for differences across states in their mean rate of firearm deaths. That is, we varied the extent to which the causal effect is indicated solely through longitudinal variation in the outcome within states or whether it is indicated by both longitudinal variability within state and variability across states. In the existing literature, the most common method to control for interstate variability is to include state-fixed effects in the model. This ensures that any differences in means across states are always fit by the model and cannot influence the causal effect of interest.

However, it is also relatively common for gun policy researchers who include state-fixed effects to also detrend the data within state (e.g., Aneja, Donohue, and Zhang, 2014; Moody et al., 2014; Raissian, 2016). In this type of model, each state has its own fixed effect to account for its mean, as well as a unique linear slope over time. Because the model also includes a national time trend (fit via year fixed effects), the state-specific linear trend is interpreted as the difference between the national time trend and the state trend.

Another method to control for interstate differences in the model is to include state random effects (e.g., Grambsch, 2008). Conceptually, controlling for state random effects is quite similar to controlling for state-fixed effects. However, these effects are estimated in a way that does not remove all variability across states from the data. Rather, it controls for difference in means across states only to the extent that the remaining variance across states is consistent with the variance expected from random sampling within a single homogeneous population.

Finally, some models do not control for differences in the mean rates of firearm deaths across states (e.g., Webster et al., 2004). In these models, the causal effect is identified using both variation over time within each state and variation across states. This includes models estimated using GEE methods to handle correlated observations within states. One cannot include fixed or random effects for the clustering variable (states) while still using GEE methods to estimate SEs.

Thus, the simulation looked at four ways in which variability in the mean value of the outcome across states could be handled by the models: (1) no controls, (2) random effects for states, (3) fixed effects for states, and (4) fixed effects for states plus state-specific linear trends relative to a national trend.

Inclusion of Autoregressive Effects

Some gun policy modeling includes a lagged outcome variable as a predictor, such as the firearm death rate at time $t–1$ when predicting the rate at time t for a given state (see, for example, Duwe, Kovandzic, and Moody, 2002; Kovandzic, Marvell, and Vieraitis, 2005; Ludwig and Cook, 2000; Moody et al., 2014; Sen and Panjamapirom, 2012). These are sometimes referred to as lagged, simplex, or Markov models (Jöreskog, 1970). Including this autoregressive predictor creates a "change" model in which the law's effect is indicated by the extent to which the firearm death rate in a given year is higher or lower than expected given the prior year's rate in the same state. Such a model is closely related to first-differences models in which one first subtracts the prior value from each value in an outcome series to create a change score, then models those change scores rather than the original variable. Indeed, when the model coefficient on the autoregressive effect equals one, the autoregressive model is exactly equivalent to a first-differences (or change-score) model. The advantage of an autoregressive model relative to a first-differences model is that the former allows for the possibility of regression to the mean, which is the tendency for extreme observations to be followed by observations that are somewhat less extreme. Autoregressive models of state firearm death rates tend to have autoregressive coefficients near 0.9, suggesting the data show some regression to the mean; the best expectation for the death rate of a given state is not exactly the same as the rate observed in the prior year but a value approximately 10 percent closer to the national average death rate than what was observed in the prior year.

Autoregressive models are popular because they correspond to relatively common hypothesized data-generating mechanisms; however, they can be difficult to work with and to interpret. Early work with autoregressive models (e.g., Cochrane and Orcutt, 1949) demonstrated that effect size estimates can be substantially biased in such models. Because of this, the coding of the predictor needs to take into account the biasing effect of the autoregressive relationship. This bias occurs because controlling for the prior value of the outcome often indirectly controls for exactly the effect the researcher is trying to measure. For example, if a law passed in 2000 has a certain effect on firearm death rates in 2005, an autoregressive model will carry that effect forward into 2006 via the autoregressive path even if the model does not include a direct effect of the law on 2006 death rates in the effect coding.

To address this possible source of bias, we investigated two types of variable coding in all models that included autoregressive effects: standard *effect coding* versus *change coding*. Standard effect coding uses the same version of the predictor variable (the simulated laws) that was used in the nonautoregressive models: The variable is coded one for each year in which the law was in place for all 12 months, zero for years when the law was never in effect, or a fractional value when it was in effect for part of a year or was in its phase-in period. Our review of the existing literature on the effect of state gun laws (RAND Corporation,

2018) found no evidence that gun policy studies that incorporate an autoregressive term have used anything other than this standard effect coding of the laws.

We also investigated *change coding*, which is the type of variable coding that is used when estimating first-difference (or change) models (Wooldridge, 2010). Change coding reflects the extent to which the hypothetical effect of the law changed since the prior year. The change coding value for the law in a given year, t, is equal to the effect coding value for the prior year minus the effect coding value for year t. Because an autoregressive model is analyzing year-over-year change in the outcome, we predict it with year-over-year change in the hypothesized effect of the law. Table 2.2 shows an example of how effect coding and change coding differ for a state implementing a new law at the beginning of 2000—for effects with an instantaneous effect and for effects that phase in over five years.

In summary, the simulation compared three options with regard to autoregressive effects within the models: (1) models without an autoregressive effect, (2) models with an autoregressive effect using standard effect coding, and (3) models with an autoregressive effect using change coding. When including the autoregressive parameter, 1979 is dropped as an outcome year (as the beginning of the data series, it lacks a lagged value). Thus, autoregressive models analyze 35 years of outcome data, while nonautoregressive models use 36 years. This

Table 2.2
Comparison of Variables Using Effect Coding and Change Coding of Laws

Type of Effect	1998	1999	2000	2001	2002	2003	2004	2005	2006
Law with an immediate effect									
Effect coding	0	0	1	1	1	1	1	1	1
Change coding	0	0	1	0	0	0	0	0	0
Law with a five-year phase-in									
Effect coding	0	0	0.1	0.3	0.5	0.7	0.9	1	1
Change coding	0	0	0.1	0.2	0.2	0.2	0.2	0.1	0

is a realistic constraint for the autoregressive models in situations in which the researcher wishes to model the data series from its beginning. However, if the researcher chooses a starting year for modeling that is not the beginning of the data series, both types of models would have the same number of usable outcome values, and the autoregressive models would have slightly more power (relative to nonautoregressive models) than is estimated in the simulation. Finally, autoregressive effects can be included in models regardless of whether state-fixed or random effects are also included and can be incorporated in both linear and log-link models. When including an autoregressive effect in models using a log-link function, the lagged variable was the log of the firearm death rate from the prior year (not the firearm death count from the prior year) to account for the effect of the population offset and the nonlinear link function used in those models.

Use of Population Weights

Researchers using linear models often weight state observations by their relative populations when fitting the models (see, for example, Durlauf, Navarro, and Rivers, 2016; Gius, 2015a, 2015b; Ludwig and Cook, 2000; Raissian, 2016). Using population weights in state-level analyses of the rate of firearm deaths results in models for which each firearm death is treated as equally important in the estimates regardless of which state it occurred in, and the overall sample characteristics are nationally representative. Alternatively, unweighted analyses could be used so that each state, rather than each person, is treated as equally important. This results in an estimation in which a death in Wyoming has nearly 100 times the effect on model parameters as a death in California, and the sample is unrepresentative of the nation in several ways (e.g., the analyses are conducted in a sample that is far more rural and white than the country actually is). This could lead to biases in estimates if either the probability of implementing the law or the effect of the law is associated with state characteristics. In the current simulation, the true effects are constant across all states regardless of size or other characteristics, so weighting is not expected to bias the asymptotic values of the effect estimates. However, choices about weighting may have substantial effects on both the true variance of those effect estimates and their modeled SEs. This is because linear models assume that the firearm death rates for all states and years are measured with homogeneous error, in spite of the fact that they are estimated on samples of different sizes. Using weights increases the influence of the largest states—those that are likely to have the most-accurate estimated rates—on model parameters. This is likely to result in model parameters that are estimated with less error and also to reduce the estimated SEs of those parameters, possibly underestimating the true SEs when applied to data from smaller states.

Across the simulations, we varied whether the state data are weighted by standardized population size (population divided by the standard deviation in population sizes across all years) when estimating linear models. These weights were treated as importance weights, not survey weights, within the analyses. Log-link models are usually conducted directly on the counts, rather than the rates, of firearm deaths and do not need to be weighted to be representative of the country.[1]

Adjustments to Standard Errors

The simulations also explored the impact of various methods for estimating SEs. For each model run, we estimated the SE in four ways: (1) the normal method implied by the chosen likelihood function, (2) robust estimators (also known as sandwich estimators, or Huber-corrected estimates) that attempt to adjust the SE for violations of distributional assumptions (White, 1980; Zeileis, 2004), (3) cluster adjustments that attempt to adjust the SE for violations of the assumed independence of observations within states (Arellano, 1987; Zeileis, 2006), and (4) estimates that apply both cluster and robust adjustments to SEs. Prior simulation studies (Aneja, Donohue, and Zhang, 2014; Helland and Tabarrok, 2004) suggest that, at least for one type of model, cluster adjustments are critical for reducing type 1 error rates to closer to the nominal value, such as $\alpha = 0.05$. However, it is not known which type of models benefit from these adjustments, whether such adjustments are sufficient to avoid excessive type 1 errors, and

---

[1]   Although rare, one recent study in this literature used a log-link model estimated on a rate outcome rather than on counts (Siegel et al., 2017). Such a model makes unusual assumptions about the error distribution and is not investigated in this current study.

whether there are conditions in which these adjustments may degrade statistical inference.

We also investigated estimating the model using GEE methods to account for variance inflation caused by nonindependents of observations within states. This is another method to account for violations of the independence assumption that has been used to estimate the effects of gun laws (e.g., Webster et al., 2004). A limitation of this approach is that it cannot be used with state-fixed or random effects. When using GEE estimation, we specified a first-order autoregressive structure to the observations within each state.

Simulation Implementation

The simulation was implemented in the R statistical programming language (version 3.3.2). The core code for running these simulations is downloadable from RAND.[2] Analyses were run using base R packages, except (a) random effect models were fit using the *LME4* package; (b) GEE models were fit using *geepack*; (c) negative binomial models were fit using the *MASS* package; and (d) SE adjustments were computed in the *sandwich* package.

In many cases, we factorially combined the model features being varied. For example, we used all types of SE estimation for both weighted and unweighted models and for models both with and without state-fixed effects. However, some possible combinations of features were omitted from the simulation because they could not be implemented in R. For example, we did not assess negative binomial models with either random effects or GEE estimation. The combination of models and model features we examined resulted in more than 100 different methods of testing for an effect of laws on death rates. Each was assessed using 90,000 simulations that varied the size and direction of the true effect, the number of states that implemented the law, and whether the law's effect had an instant or five-year phase-in period.

---

[2] The core code is available on the product page of this report on the RAND Corporation's website.

CHAPTER THREE

Results

Type 1 Error Rates

Table 3.1 shows the type 1 error rates across a wide range of models and SE estimation methods. To simplify presentation, several models and estimation methods have been omitted from this table. In particular, Poisson models were not included because they always performed worse than the corresponding negative binomial models. Huber corrections for the SE were also not included for negative binomial models because they always resulted in excessive type 1 errors, and we only present results for one log-linear model (i.e., linear model of a logged outcome) to demonstrate that this transformation is not an improvement over the corresponding linear models.

Almost all of the models that are commonly used in this field demonstrate poor type 1 error rates when fit to these data. For example, the classic two-way linear fixed-effects model (i.e., standard difference-in-differences model), using population weights and without any adjustment to the SE, have an average type 1 error rate of 0.62 across the six types of simulated laws we considered (three different numbers of states by two different phase-in periods). This is 12 times the rate of false positives that are expected when using an $\alpha = 0.05$ level of significance. Even using a cluster adjustment, the best adjustment to SEs for this model, the average type 1 error rate is 0.20, still four times higher than the claimed false positive rate.

Somewhat surprisingly, the SE adjustments often made the type 1 error worse, although, in some cases, clustering adjustments did reduce these errors. Generally, all of the models with state-fixed effects and no

Table 3.1
Type 1 Error Rates for Each Model, by Number of Implementing States and Length of Phase-in Period

Model Type	Autoregression Effect	State Effect	SE Adjustment	Instant Phase-in (No. of States)			Five-Year Phase-in (No. of States)			Average	Worst
				3	15	35	3	15	35		
Negative binomial	Change	None	None	0.04	0.04	0.04	0.03	0.02	0.02	**0.03**	**0.02***[*]
Negative binomial	Change	None	Cluster	0.23	0.09	0.07	0.22	0.08	0.06	0.12	0.23
Negative binomial	Effect	None	None	0.10	0.10	0.09	0.10	0.10	0.10	0.10	0.10[*]
Negative binomial	Effect	None	Cluster	0.22	0.12	0.11	0.23	0.13	0.12	0.15	0.23
Negative binomial	Change	Fixed	None	0.06	0.05	0.06	0.09	0.11	0.13	**0.08**	**0.13**[*]
Negative binomial	Change	Fixed	Cluster	0.22	0.09	0.07	0.21	0.09	0.09	0.13	0.22
Negative binomial	Effect	Fixed	None	0.19	0.28	0.26	0.21	0.30	0.27	0.25	0.30
Negative binomial	Effect	Fixed	Cluster	0.21	0.12	0.11	0.21	0.13	0.11	0.15	0.21[*]
Negative binomial	None	Fixed	None	0.48	0.53	0.51	0.50	0.56	0.53	0.52	0.56
Negative binomial	None	Fixed	Cluster	0.19	0.09	0.07	0.20	0.09	0.07	0.12	0.20[*]
Negative binomial	None	Fixed and trend	None	0.37	0.39	0.41	0.41	0.44	0.44	0.41	0.44
Negative binomial	None	Fixed and trend	Cluster	0.24	0.10	0.08	0.24	0.11	0.08	0.14	0.24[*]

Table 3.1—Continued

Model Type	Autoregression Effect	State Effect	SE Adjustment	Instant Phase-in (No. of States)			Five-Year Phase-in (No. of States)				
				3	15	35	3	15	35	Average	Worst
Log linear-weighted	None	Fixed	None	0.52	0.70	0.70	0.54	0.73	0.71	0.65	0.73
Log linear-weighted	None	Fixed	Huber	0.59	0.66	0.62	0.61	0.69	0.64	0.64	0.69
Log linear-weighted	None	Fixed	Cluster	0.28	0.18	0.16	0.29	0.18	0.16	0.21	0.29*
Log linear-weighted	None	Fixed	Both	0.58	0.65	0.61	0.60	0.68	0.63	0.63	0.68
Linear-weighted	Change	None	None	0.07	0.09	0.10	0.07	0.11	0.10	**0.09**	0.11*
Linear-weighted	Change	None	Huber	0.22	0.10	0.08	0.08	0.08	0.07	0.10	0.22
Linear-weighted	Change	None	Cluster	0.30	0.12	0.09	0.27	0.13	0.10	0.17	0.30
Linear-weighted	Change	None	Both	0.21	0.09	0.07	0.08	0.08	0.06	0.10	0.21
Linear-weighted	Effect	None	None	0.12	0.16	0.16	0.11	0.16	0.16	0.15	0.16
Linear-weighted	Effect	None	Huber	0.13	0.16	0.14	0.13	0.17	0.16	0.15	0.17
Linear-weighted	Effect	None	Cluster	0.28	0.19	0.16	0.27	0.19	0.17	0.21	0.28
Linear-weighted	Effect	None	Both	0.13	0.15	0.13	0.13	0.16	0.15	0.14	0.16*

Table 3.1—Continued

Model Type	Autoregression Effect	State Effect	SE Adjustment	Instant Phase-in (No. of States)			Five-Year Phase-in (No. of States)			Average	Worst
				3	15	35	3	15	35		
Linear–weighted	Change	Fixed	None	0.09	0.11	0.12	0.11	0.18	0.21	0.14	0.21*
Linear–weighted	Change	Fixed	Huber	0.22	0.12	0.09	0.12	0.16	0.18	0.15	0.22
Linear–weighted	Change	Fixed	Cluster	0.28	0.13	0.09	0.25	0.14	0.13	0.17	0.28
Linear–weighted	Change	Fixed	Both	0.21	0.11	0.09	0.11	0.15	0.16	0.14	0.21
Linear–weighted	Effect	Fixed	None	0.20	0.33	0.32	0.22	0.35	0.33	0.29	0.35
Linear–weighted	Effect	Fixed	Huber	0.20	0.30	0.27	0.22	0.32	0.29	0.27	0.32
Linear–weighted	Effect	Fixed	Cluster	0.27	0.20	0.16	0.27	0.20	0.16	0.21	0.27*
Linear–weighted	Effect	Fixed	Both	0.19	0.28	0.26	0.21	0.30	0.27	0.25	0.30
Linear–weighted	Change	Random	None	0.08	0.09	0.10	0.07	0.10	0.11	**0.09**	0.11*
Linear–weighted	Effect	Random	None	0.09	0.11	0.10	0.09	0.11	0.10	0.10	0.11*
Linear–weighted	None	None	GEE	0.28	0.12	0.10	0.29	0.13	0.10	0.17	0.29*
Linear–weighted	None	Fixed	None	0.55	0.66	0.64	0.56	0.68	0.66	0.62	0.68
Linear–weighted	None	Fixed	Huber	0.58	0.61	0.56	0.60	0.63	0.59	0.60	0.63
Linear–weighted	None	Fixed	Cluster	0.29	0.17	0.16	0.29	0.17	0.15	0.20	0.29*

Table 3.1—Continued

Model Type	Autoregression Effect	State Effect	SE Adjustment	Instant Phase-in (No. of States)			Five-Year Phase-in (No. of States)			Average	Worst
				3	15	35	3	15	35		
Linear-weighted	None	Fixed	Both	0.57	0.60	0.55	0.59	0.62	0.58	0.59	0.62
Linear-weighted	None	Fixed and trend	None	0.43	0.51	0.53	0.47	0.55	0.55	0.51	0.55
Linear-weighted	None	Fixed and trend	Huber	0.44	0.46	0.46	0.49	0.51	0.49	0.48	0.51
Linear-weighted	None	Fixed and trend	Cluster	0.29	0.16	0.13	0.30	0.16	0.13	0.19	0.30*
Linear-weighted	None	Fixed and trend	Both	0.42	0.44	0.44	0.47	0.49	0.47	0.46	0.49
Linear-unweighted	Change	None	None	0.04	0.04	0.04	0.01	0.01	0.01	**0.02**	0.01*
Linear-unweighted	Change	None	Huber	0.14	0.05	0.04	0.04	0.02	0.01	0.05	0.14
Linear-unweighted	Change	None	Cluster	0.20	0.07	0.06	0.17	0.07	0.05	0.10	0.20
Linear-unweighted	Change	None	Both	0.14	0.05	0.04	0.04	0.01	0.01	0.05	0.14
Linear-unweighted	Effect	None	None	0.06	0.05	0.05	0.06	0.05	0.05	**0.05**	0.06*
Linear-unweighted	Effect	None	Huber	0.11	0.08	0.07	0.10	0.08	0.07	0.08	0.11
Linear-unweighted	Effect	None	Cluster	0.16	0.09	0.09	0.16	0.10	0.09	0.11	0.16

Table 3.1—Continued

Model Type	Autoregression Effect	State Effect	SE Adjustment	Instant Phase-in (No. of States)			Five-Year Phase-in (No. of States)			Average	Worst
				3	15	35	3	15	35		
Linear–unweighted	Effect	None	Both	0.10	0.07	0.06	0.10	0.08	0.06	0.08	0.10
Linear–unweighted	Change	Fixed	None	0.05	0.05	0.04	0.07	0.05	0.06	**0.05**	0.07*
Linear–unweighted	Change	Fixed	Huber	0.16	0.08	0.06	0.10	0.07	0.07	0.09	0.16
Linear–unweighted	Change	Fixed	Cluster	0.20	0.07	0.06	0.17	0.07	0.06	0.11	0.20
Linear–unweighted	Change	Fixed	Both	0.14	0.07	0.05	0.10	0.06	0.06	0.08	0.14
Linear–unweighted	Effect	Fixed	None	0.17	0.16	0.14	0.18	0.19	0.15	0.17	0.19
Linear–unweighted	Effect	Fixed	Huber	0.21	0.19	0.16	0.24	0.21	0.17	0.20	0.24
Linear–unweighted	Effect	Fixed	Cluster	0.17	0.08	0.07	0.17	0.09	0.06	0.11	0.17*
Linear–unweighted	Effect	Fixed	Both	0.20	0.18	0.14	0.22	0.20	0.16	0.18	0.22
Linear–unweighted	Change	Random	None	0.05	0.04	0.04	0.04	0.03	0.03	**0.04**	0.03*
Linear–unweighted	Effect	Random	None	0.12	0.12	0.09	0.13	0.13	0.10	0.11	0.13*
Linear–unweighted	None	None	GEE	0.21	0.08	0.07	0.19	0.08	0.06	0.11	0.21*
Linear–unweighted	None	Fixed	None	0.45	0.46	0.41	0.47	0.48	0.44	0.45	0.48
Linear–unweighted	None	Fixed	Huber	0.49	0.47	0.42	0.52	0.50	0.46	0.47	0.52

Table 3.1—Continued

Model Type	Autoregression Effect	State Effect	SE Adjustment	Instant Phase-in (No. of States)			Five-Year Phase-in (No. of States)			Average	Worst
				3	15	35	3	15	35		
Linear–unweighted	None	Fixed	Cluster	0.18	0.09	0.07	0.18	0.10	0.07	0.12	0.18*
Linear–unweighted	None	Fixed	Both	0.48	0.46	0.40	0.51	0.48	0.44	0.46	0.51
Linear–unweighted	None	Fixed and trend	None	0.29	0.31	0.33	0.31	0.36	0.37	0.33	0.37
Linear–unweighted	None	Fixed and trend	Huber	0.34	0.33	0.34	0.37	0.38	0.38	0.35	0.38
Linear–unweighted	None	Fixed and trend	Cluster	0.19	0.08	0.07	0.18	0.08	0.07	0.11	0.19*
Linear–unweighted	None	Fixed and trend	Both	0.32	0.31	0.31	0.35	0.36	0.36	0.33	0.36

NOTES: All tests conducted with $\alpha = 0.05$. *Average* (in header row) refers to the average type 1 error rate over the six simulation conditions for each model. *Worst* refers to the type 1 error rate that was most discrepant from the intended 0.05 rate of false positives. Bold indicates that average type 1 error rates for the preferred method were less than 0.10. Asterisk indicates the preferred method of computing SEs for each model.

autoregressive effects benefited from a cluster adjustment, while SEs for models with autoregressive effects and without state-fixed effects were often worse when a cluster adjustment was applied. The cluster adjustment made little difference for models with both autoregressive effects and state-fixed effects. In contrast, applying the so-called robust SEs almost always resulted in worse type 1 error rates, sometimes substantially worse. This was particularly true whenever the estimate benefited from a clustering adjustment.

For each model type, we identified the best method for computing the SE. This was done by first computing a correction factor that, when applied to the computed SE, yielded a 0.05 type 1 error rate in the simulation. The preferred method of computing the SE was identified by the correction factor that is closest to one within the law condition that required the largest correction factor.[1] That is, we selected the least bad method of computing the SE and highlight this model in our discussion concerning correct rejection rates. The correction factors for all models are included in Appendix B. The estimates from the preferred SE-correction method are also indicated with an asterisk in Table 3.1. Looking at the 25 preferred methods for calculating SEs, only one involved a Huber correction, and the advantage of the Huber correction over the corresponding ordinary SE was small. Given this, researchers should be quite cautious about using so-called robust SEs with longitudinal data such as these, at least any time the robust SEs are actually smaller than the SEs without the robustness correction.

Overall, only a few models came plausibly close to the intended 0.05 false-positive rate across the six law conditions we simulated. Using the preferred SE-correction method, only eight of 25 models had average type 1 error rates of less than 0.10—that is, twice the intended rate. All eight of these models included an autoregressive effect, and none of them applied either a cluster adjustment or Huber adjustment to the SEs. Additionally, seven of those eight autoregressive models used the *change coded* version of the law, rather than the more common *effect coded* version.

---

[1]   The best correction factor was the one that had the lowest value of $(cf - 1)^2$, where cf is the correction factor.

Several broad patterns emerge within these results. Within a given link function, *change coded* autoregressive models typically had slightly fewer false positives than the corresponding *effect coded* autoregressive models, which had fewer false positives than the corresponding models without an autoregressive effect (but with a cluster adjustment). However, the difference between these classes of models varied greatly as a function of the number of states that implemented the simulated laws. The models without an autoregressive effect had dramatically more false positives when only three states implemented the law, slightly fewer false positives when 15 states implemented, and only a few more when 35 states implemented. As was shown in other simulations, difference-in-differences models with an autoregressive data series require some adjustment for clustering. However, none of the standard adjustments worked unless the number of treated units (states) was moderately large (Bertrand, Duflo, and Mullainathan, 2004). With the current data, the false-positive rate for these models using the clustering adjustment improves dramatically, from three to 35 treated states, but never reaches the correct 0.05 level. In contrast, several of the autoregressive models have false positives at, or slightly under, 0.05 in the same condition.

The rate of type 1 errors also varied somewhat as a function of model type or link function. In general, the negative binomial and the unweighted linear model both performed similarly and both had fewer false positives than their corresponding weighted linear models. Giving greater weight to the largest states with the best-estimated death rates appears to result in underestimated SEs when using a linear model. The use of log-linear models (linear models run on logged outcomes) did not improve the performance of the corresponding linear models. This is likely because the residuals of the models are approximately normally distributed when the counts of deaths within a given state-year tend to be relatively high. It is plausible that, with an outcome where observed values are closer to the zero bound (e.g., child firearm homicides), such a transformation, or the use of Huber-corrected SEs, may have been beneficial rather than harmful.

The rate of type 1 errors varied little as a function of inclusion of state effects. Within autoregressive models, adding state random effects had almost no effect. This is likely because the state random effects, conditioned on the autoregressive effect, were all approximately zero in these data. Adding state-fixed effects to the autoregressive models slightly increased the type 1 error rate, regardless of link function. Similarly, the GEE models without state or autoregressive effects had very slightly less type 1 error than the cluster-adjusted model that included state-fixed effects.

Overall, this simulation illustrates how difficult it is to properly characterize the statistical uncertainty of causal effect estimates derived from state-year time-series data. The demonstrated bias in the SEs was almost entirely in the anticonservative direction, with the vast majority of methods resulting in more than 10-percent false positives, twice the correct rate, while there was only one with a corresponding conservative error of less than 2.5-percent false positives, or half the correct rate. To keep the rate of false positives to a reasonable level (e.g., between 7.5 percent and 2.5 percent when hypothesis testing using $p < 0.05$) across the full range of laws, we are limited to autoregressive models using *change coding* that is estimated as either an unweighted linear model or a negative binomial model. In cases in which the law in question has been adopted by a clear majority of states, there may be nearly appropriate inferences using the nonautoregressive models. Even then, the inferences will be somewhat anticonservative even when applying an SE correction for clustering.

Correct Rejection Rates

Having the correct false-positive rate suggests that the estimated SE of the effect in question is appropriately calibrated to the true statistical uncertainty in the estimate. We also want to look across these models at the true statistical uncertainty of the estimates. Even if two models are similar in their rates of false positives, one of them may be much more precise or efficient in estimating the effect, allowing for greater probability of rejecting the null hypothesis when it is, in fact, not true. In this section, we present the power of these models to detect a true effect. More specifically, we estimate the correct rejection rate that is the proportion of the simulations under an alternative hypothesis in which the model rejects the null hypothesis and the coefficient is in the same direction as the true effect. When computing the rate of correct rejection for a given model, we base those statistical tests on the method of computing the SE that displayed the best type 1 error characteristics (marked with an asterisk in Table 3.1).

However, it is impossible to accurately compare correct rejection rates across models that use different effective levels of significance. It is always possible to make more-correct rejections if one is willing to accept more false positives. Thus, to compare models, we start by using the preferred SEs for each model and then apply the SE correction factor for that condition of the simulation (see Table A.1 in Appendix A), which results in exactly 5-percent false positives across the null hypothesis simulations we performed for the model. Thus, all comparisons of correct rejection rates are made at a true 5-percent false positive rate, even though achieving this false-positive rate sometimes requires substantial corrections even to the adjusted SEs. Using this correction procedure for significance testing, we compute the adjusted correct rejection rate across simulated data sets (see Table 3.2).

Across all six of the simulated law conditions (three being the number of states implementing by two lengths of effect phase-in), these models have extremely low power to detect an effect of a law that causes or prevents 1,000 deaths per year nationally. Good power is normally considered to be 0.8, lower power is considered to be 0.5, and anything below approximately 0.2 is considered to be problematic (Cohen, 1988). A scientific field built on studies with such low power (e.g., less than 0.20) will have a large fraction of significant results that are spurious, a substantial proportion of significant effects that are in the wrong direction, and significant effects that substantially overestimate the true effect size (Gelman and Carlin, 2014). In fact, some of the observed rates are not much better than chance; given a 5-percent false-positive rate, we expect at least 2.5-percent rejections in each direction even without any true effect. Several models have conditions in which they have only 4-percent correct rejections, and seven of the models had average correct rejection rates below 0.10.

Table 3.2
Adjusted Correct Rejection Rates for Each Model, by Number of Implementing States and Length of Phase-in Period

Model Type	Autoregression Effect	State Effect	SE Adjustment	Instant Phase-in (No. of States)			Five-Year Phase-in (No. of States)			Average
				3	15	35	3	15	35	
Negative binomial	Change	None	None	0.08	0.27	0.50	0.05	0.12	0.22	0.21
Negative binomial	Effect	None	None	0.05	0.10	0.15	0.04	0.08	0.10	0.09
Negative binomial	Change	Fixed	None	0.06	0.20	0.37	0.04	0.06	0.10	0.14
Negative binomial	Effect	Fixed	Cluster	0.06	0.14	0.20	0.05	0.11	0.15	0.12
Negative binomial	None	Fixed	Cluster	0.07	0.16	0.24	0.06	0.14	0.19	0.14
Negative binomial	None	Fixed and trend	Cluster	0.06	0.16	0.35	0.05	0.11	0.22	0.16
Log linear–weighted	None	Fixed	Cluster	0.05	0.10	0.12	0.04	0.09	0.10	0.08
Log linear–weighted	Change	None	None	0.06	0.20	0.39	0.04	0.08	0.14	0.15
Log linear–weighted	Effect	None	Both	0.05	0.08	0.11	0.04	0.07	0.08	0.07
Log linear–weighted	Change	Fixed	None	0.05	0.16	0.29	0.03	0.05	0.08	0.11
Log linear–weighted	Effect	Fixed	Both	0.04	0.09	0.14	0.04	0.07	0.10	0.08
Log linear–weighted	Change	Random	None	0.06	0.20	0.38	0.04	0.07	0.13	0.15
Log linear–weighted	Effect	Random	None	0.05	0.09	0.14	0.04	0.08	0.09	0.08
Log linear–weighted	None	None	GEE	0.08	0.22	0.41	0.06	0.11	0.17	0.17

Table 3.2—Continued

Model Type	Autoregression Effect	State Effect	SE Adjustment	Instant Phase-in (No. of States)			Five-Year Phase-in (No. of States)			Average
				3	15	35	3	15	35	
Linear–weighted	None	Fixed	Cluster	0.06	0.09	0.13	0.05	0.08	0.11	0.09
Linear–weighted	None	Fixed and trend	Cluster	0.06	0.10	0.20	0.05	0.08	0.13	0.10
Linear–unweighted	Change	None	None	0.06	0.16	0.31	0.05	0.11	0.19	0.15
Linear–unweighted	Effect	None	None	0.06	0.13	0.18	0.05	0.11	0.14	0.11
Linear–unweighted	Change	Fixed	None	0.05	0.11	0.23	0.04	0.06	0.09	0.10
Linear–unweighted	Effect	Fixed	Cluster	0.07	0.17	0.28	0.06	0.14	0.22	0.16
Linear–unweighted	Change	Random	None	0.05	0.12	0.25	0.04	0.07	0.10	0.11
Linear–unweighted	Effect	Random	None	0.07	0.19	0.30	0.06	0.14	0.22	0.16
Linear–unweighted	None	None	GEE	0.07	0.19	0.34	0.06	0.14	0.24	0.17
Linear–unweighted	None	Fixed	Cluster	0.06	0.15	0.26	0.06	0.13	0.21	0.14
Linear–unweighted	None	Fixed and trend	Cluster	0.06	0.17	0.32	0.06	0.12	0.23	0.16

NOTES: All tests conducted with $\alpha = 0.05$. Average (in the header row) refers to the average correct rejection rate over the six simulation conditions for each model. Results are presented from the preferred method of computing SEs for each model. Results are based on a true effect size such that the law would result in an increase or decrease of 1,000 deaths nationwide in an average year. Rates are averaged over positive and negative effects.

Against this backdrop of extremely low power, some models did considerably better than others. The best model was the negative binomial autoregressive change coding, which had an average correct rejection rate of 0.21. This was followed by the two GEE linear models at 0.17.

The clearest pattern in the data is that power increases with the number of states that implemented the law. Across all models and phase-in periods, the average correct rejection rates are 0.05, 0.12, and 0.21 for three, 15, and 35 state conditions, respectively. The correct rejection rate is also somewhat higher when the phase-in is instant (0.16) than when it occurs over five years (0.10).

There are also several patterns in correct rejection rates among the model features. Adding state-fixed effects typically resulted in slightly less power relative to the corresponding model without those fixed effects. This is to be expected because state-fixed effects are correlated with the law-effect variable within a state unless the implementation date happens to be in the middle of the study period. Similarly, *effect coded* autoregressive models generally have slightly less power than those using *change coding*.

The negative binomial autoregressive change coding model had the best power (0.21) and also had especially good average type 1 error rates (0.03) without any adjustments or corrections. Of the eight models that showed a type 1 error of less than 0.10, the negative binomial autoregressive change coding model had the highest correct rejection rate within each of the six law conditions included in the simulation. Among those eight models, the next best power was for the linear weighted autoregressive change coding model (0.15), followed by the linear unweighted autoregressive change coding model (also 0.15). Thus, among the models with marginally acceptable false-positive rates, the three models that offered the most power to identify a true effect were all autoregressive change code models without state-fixed effects. They differed only in whether they were estimated as negative binomial, weighted linear, or unweighted linear. The negative binomial version offered slightly better performance on both type 1 error and the rate of correct rejections relative to the two linear models, and this was true within each of the six law conditions we investigated. However, even this "best" model had unacceptably low power when evaluated at an effect size of 1,000 additional deaths per year nationally, at least when fewer than 35 states had implemented the law.

Directional Bias

Table 3.3 shows directional bias in the effect estimates for each model. This is computed using the simulation runs in which there is either a true positive effect or a true negative effect of equal size. Directional bias assesses the extent to which the estimate favors a positive (increases in death) or negative (decreases in death) effect, in spite of the fact that both of these true effects are the same size. To facilitate comparisons across both log and linear models, we converted all bias measures into linear units and expressed them in the number of deaths. The true effect sizes for the positive and negative conditions are either plus or minus 1,000 deaths if the policy were applied nationally in an average year. Thus, a model that estimates the effects as +1,100 and −900 for the positive and negative conditions, respectively, would have a directional bias of 100.[2]

For almost all of the models, directional bias was descriptively small (e.g., bias smaller than plus or minus 40 deaths) relative to the true effect of 1,000 deaths and very small relative to the actual number of deaths annually (approximately 30,000). This level of bias was also

---

[2] Converting all bias metrics into linear units (a count of deaths) provides a small advantage to the linear models when making comparisons to nonlinear models because this metric is directly proportional to the model coefficients in a linear model. Thus, the value of this bias metric is zero any time the model parameter is unbiased. In contrast, this bias metric is proportional to the exponentiated model coefficients for the log-link models. Thus, it is possible that a negative binomial model that has unbiased model coefficients in their native units will show a small bias on the exponentiated coefficients. There is no method to compare bias across linear and nonlinear models that allows both to be in their native units. If all directional and magnitude bias measures are converted into the native units of the negative binomial models (log risk ratios), the negative binomial models tend to show slightly better performance relative to the linear models than is evident in Tables 3.3 and 3.4. We chose to present bias in linear units because we ultimately identify a negative binomial model as the best overall model and did not want to measure directional and magnitude bias in a way that could be seen as favoring that choice.

Table 3.3
Directional Bias for Each Model, by Number of Implementing States and Length of Phase-in Period

Model Type	Autoregression Effect	State Effect	Instant Phase-in (No. of States)			Five Year Phase-in (No. of States)			Average
			3	15	35	3	15	35	
Negative binomial	Change	None	-10	-4	10	48	19	24	14
Negative binomial	Effect	None	-15	-4	-1	-16	-4	-2	-7
Negative binomial	Change	Fixed	13	3	11	285	71	41	71
Negative binomial	Effect	Fixed	17	-1	3	12	-3	1	5
Negative binomial	None	Fixed	84	12	22	86	11	24	40
Negative binomial	None	Fixed and trend	52	11	7	71	20	9	28
Log linear–weighted	None	Fixed	532	135	71	610	149	73	262
Linear–weighted	Change	None	14	1	17	74	7	43	26
Linear–weighted	Effect	None	30	7	3	34	8	1	14
Linear–weighted	Change	Fixed	-2	1	17	10	-4	46	11
Linear–weighted	Effect	Fixed	85	17	8	89	16	3	36
Linear–weighted	Change	Random	-3	0	17	28	5	42	15
Linear–weighted	Effect	Random	29	7	3	36	9	0	14
Linear–weighted	None	None/GEE	193	37	19	476	82	25	139

Table 3.3—Continued

Model Type	Autoregression Effect	State Effect	Instant Phase-in (No. of States)			Five Year Phase-in (No. of States)			
			3	15	35	3	15	35	Average
Linear-weighted	None	Fixed	313	62	31	340	61	19	138
Linear-weighted	None	Fixed and trend	13	6	1	-11	3	-6	1
Linear-unweighted	Change	None	-36	-4	16	-48	-7	13	-11
Linear-unweighted	Effect	None	-6	1	-1	-4	2	-2	-2
Linear-unweighted	Change	Fixed	-2	7	22	17	19	28	15
Linear-unweighted	Effect	Fixed	-5	0	2	-9	-2	-2	-3
Linear-unweighted	Change	Random	-12	3	20	0	11	24	8
Linear-unweighted	Effect	Random	-7	1	2	-9	0	-2	-3
Linear-unweighted	None	None/GEE	-28	-6	14	-27	-5	-2	-9
Linear-unweighted	None	Fixed	-9	-1	8	-23	-7	0	-5
Linear-unweighted	None	Fixed and trend	10	-9	6	-2	-9	-1	-1

NOTES: Effect sizes were scaled as a count of deaths if the law were implemented and fully phased in nationally in an average year. Positive directional bias numbers indicate bias toward finding that the policy increases deaths, while negative numbers indicate bias toward finding that the policy decreases deaths. The true effects used in the simulations were plus or minus 1,000 deaths for the positive and negative conditions, respectively. Average (in the header row) refers to the average directional bias over the six simulation conditions for each model.

small relative to the variance of the estimates, generally more than an order of magnitude smaller, and thus it likely contributed minimally to the overall error of the estimates (e.g., the total error expressed as the root mean SE). However, three models showed moderate directional bias of greater than +100 deaths averaged across conditions, suggesting a bias for those models toward finding that laws increased deaths. The worst of these was the linear model with a log-transformed death rate as the outcome, which was biased by an average of +262 deaths. This could occur, for example, if the true error distribution was substantially skewed relative to the assumptions of the model, yielding nonsymmetrical errors under the null hypothesis. None of the three models that showed moderate bias had acceptable type 1 error or good correct rejection rates and thus were not under consideration as an appropriate model.

The one clear pattern in the directional bias findings is that measurable directional bias occurs primarily in the three state conditions, except for those three models that showed moderate directional bias on average. This difference across conditions likely occurs because the error in the estimated effect may be highly symmetrical when a large number of states are averaged together due to the central limit theorem, even if the errors in the effect for individual states are highly skewed. Researchers who attempt to estimate effects for a small number of states (or even one state) should recognize the potential for substantial bias if the model is not chosen carefully.

Magnitude Bias

Table 3.4 shows magnitude bias across the various models and conditions of the simulation. Such bias represents the extent to which the estimate is less extreme than the true effect (negative magnitude bias) or more extreme than the true effect (positive magnitude bias).[3] Such

---

[3]   The magnitude bias is computed as the magnitude of all of the estimated effects, regardless of statistical significance. If one interprets only effects that are statistically significant, almost all models will overestimate the true magnitude of the effect, with models that have lower power showing greater magnitude bias. This is because almost all simulated samples

Table 3.4
Magnitude Bias for Each Model, by Number of Implementing States and Length of Phase-in Period

Model Type	Autoregression Effect	State Effect	Instant Phase-in (No. of States)			Five Year Phase-in (No. of States)			Average	Percentage of True Effects
			3	15	35	3	15	35		
Negative binomial	Change	None	3	–10	–32	165	116	30	45	5
Negative binomial	Effect	None	–855	–854	–846	–863	–866	–870	–859	–86
Negative binomial	Change	Fixed	–188	–181	–172	–121	–126	–142	–155	–15
Negative binomial	Effect	Fixed	–634	–625	–608	–652	–651	–646	–636	–64
Negative binomial	None	Fixed	3	1	2	4	2	2	2	0
Negative binomial	None	Fixed and trend	3	1	1	5	2	2	2	0
Log linear–weighted	None	Fixed	16	4	2	19	5	2	8	1
Log linear–weighted	Change	None	–2	–16	–33	127	80	9	28	3
Log linear–weighted	Effect	None	–869	–868	–859	–876	–881	–884	–873	–87

Table 3.4—Continued

Model Type	Autoregression Effect	State Effect	Instant Phase-in (No. of States)			Five Year Phase-in (No. of States)			Average	Percentage of True Effects
			3	15	35	3	15	35		
Log linear–weighted	Change	Fixed	-153	-143	-136	-124	-112	-119	-131	-13
Log linear–weighted	Effect	Fixed	-706	-695	-675	-728	-725	-720	-708	-71
Log linear–weighted	Change	Random	-32	-41	-50	67	29	-19	-8	-1
Linear–weighted	Effect	Random	-847	-842	-828	-858	-861	-862	-850	-85
Linear–weighted	None	None/GEE	0	0	0	0	0	0	0	0
Linear–weighted	None	Fixed	0	0	0	0	0	0	0	0
Linear–weighted	None	Fixed and trend	0	0	0	0	0	0	0	0
Linear–unweighted	Change	None	4	-17	-52	249	175	38	66	7
Linear–unweighted	Effect	None	-802	-801	-793	-809	-812	-816	-805	-81
Linear–unweighted	Change	Fixed	-261	-249	-238	-182	-179	-203	-219	-22

Table 3.4—Continued

Model Type	Autoregression Effect	State Effect	Instant Phase-in (No. of States)			Five Year Phase-in (No. of States)			Average	Percentage of True Effects
			3	15	35	3	15	35		
Linear–unweighted	Effect	Fixed	-515	-509	-495	-531	-529	-526	-517	-52
Linear–unweighted	Change	Random	-225	-216	-207	-146	-147	-174	-186	-19
Linear–unweighted	Effect	Random	-568	-562	-546	-585	-584	-580	-571	-57
Linear–unweighted	None	None/GEE	0	0	0	0	0	0	0	0
Linear–unweighted	None	Fixed	0	0	0	0	0	0	0	0
Linear–unweighted	None	Fixed and trend	0	0	0	0	0	0	0	0

NOTES: Effect sizes were scaled as a count of deaths if the law were implemented and fully phased in nationally in an average year. Positive magnitude bias numbers indicate that the estimated number of deaths were more extreme than the true number of deaths, while negative numbers indicate that the estimated number of deaths had a smaller absolute magnitude than the true number of deaths. *Average* (in header row) refers to the average magnitude bias over the six simulation conditions for each model. *Percentage of true effects* scales the average bias as a function of the true effect magnitude (1,000 deaths).

bias is not necessarily a threat to the validity of the statistical inference from standard hypothesis testing, but it makes it hard to correctly estimate the practical importance of the law. This type of bias could be seen as analogous to instances in which an effect is measured in measurement units other than the expected units.

The distribution of magnitude bias within our simulations was bimodal, with most models having negligible magnitude bias (e.g., estimated effects that were plus or minus 10 percent of the true effect). Nonetheless, some models had substantial negative bias such that the average estimated effect was less than half the magnitude of the true effect size. The models that showed such large biases were the autoregressive ones that used effect coding for the law. Averaged across these models, they underestimated the true effect by 73 percent; that is, the true effect was four times larger than the estimated effect. Autoregressive models using change coding could also show nontrivial magnitude bias when state-fixed effects were added to the model. Across the various model types, these models underestimated the magnitude of the true effect by an average of 17 percent.

The negative binomial autoregressive change code model that was favored on the basis of its type 1 error and correct rejection rate has relatively modest magnitude bias, overestimating the effect size by an average of 5 percent across all conditions. Again, this is largely because of the three-state condition. Looking at the 15 and 35 state conditions, the magnitude bias is less than 3 percent of the true effect.

Other Considerations in Model Selection

The primary purpose of the simulation was to identify the statistical performance of various methods of estimating an effect and testing it for significance within the state-by-year firearm death data. However, the four measures of statistical performance we assessed are not

---

that showed a statistically significant effect had an estimate effect that was more extreme that the true effect.

the only criteria on which to select a statistical method. For example, researchers often deliberately choose models that have lower power but offer improved causal inference. In this section, we examine other possible considerations in model selection that may qualify our findings from the simulation.

One common reason for selecting a model that has less statistical precision to estimate the effect of interest is to make the findings more robust to the biasing effects of confounding variables. A confounding variable would be one that has causal effects on both the enactment of the law and on the firearm death rate, thereby creating a spurious association between the law and the change in death rate (Kish, 1959; Greenland, Robins, and Pearl, 1999). Researchers typically add covariates to models to mitigate the potentially confounding effects of measured variables (see, for example, VanderWeele and Shpitser, 2011), or they may add state-fixed effects to the model to mitigate the potentially confounding effects of unmeasured characteristics that vary across states. Our preferred model on the basis of the simulations does not include state-fixed effects, but some may prefer to add state-fixed effects under the belief that such a model is more robust to omitted covariates, even though doing so would increase type 1 error, would decrease correct rejections, and would slightly increase both types of bias.

Within our simulations, the laws had no systematic relationship to any other variables, so there was no risk of confounding. However, model performance in the simulation may have differed if the laws had been associated with either the included covariates or omitted variables that were also associated with the firearm death rates. While it would be possible to design a different simulation that included a range of confounding variables, it is possible to more directly assess the extent to which the effect estimates from these various model types are robust to the inclusion or exclusion of specific covariates outside of a simulation. Our models include covariates that were identified in the literature as potential sources of confounding. Omitting such a covariate from a model will affect the other model parameters only to the extent it is independently associated with the outcome; that is, omitting a variable that had a regression coefficient of zero will not alter the point estimates for other coefficients in that model. In that case, the causal effect estimate is robust with respect to the exclusion of that covariate because the estimate would not change when it is omitted.[4]

More generally, for any given causal effect of a confounding variable on the probability of implementing the gun law, the magnitude of the bias that could be removed by including the variable as a covariate is proportional to its coefficient in that model (Pearl, 2009). Because of this relationship, we can determine the extent to which the causal effect estimates from the various models would be robust with respect to the omission of the 17 covariates thought to represent potential confounders, even though our simulations did not include an association between these variables and the probability of the laws being implemented. Models that rely more heavily on those variables in predicting the outcome will produce causal effect estimates that are more sensitive to their omission in any scenario in which the treatment is also associated with those variables.

Specifically, we compared five model types based on how much each relied on the covariates for prediction and thus the extent to which their causal effect estimates would be sensitive to the omission of those covariates. We looked at (1) a base model that includes fixed effects for year but without state-fixed effects or autoregressive effects, similar to a typical GEE model of the phenomena; (2) a model that adds an autoregressive effect to the base model; (3) a model that adds state-fixed effects to the base model; (4) a model that adds both an autoregressive effect and state-fixed effects to the base model; and (5) a model that adds state-fixed effects and state-specific linear trends to the base model. For each model, we can fit a version in which we omit all covariates, as well as a second version in which we include all covariates (17 orthogonal principal components derived from the 36 vari-

---

[4]   Determining whether the inclusion of a given measured covariate will alter a causal effect estimate is not the same as determining which specific variables are potential confounds. The latter determination is inherently based on the underlying causal structure of the phenomena and cannot be directly inferred from associations in the data (Pearl, 2009). For the purposes of this report, the set of variables that are exemplars of expected confounds is derived from the published theory and empirical research on the effects of gun laws. These are represented in the 17 included covariates. The current analyses are designed to determine the extent to which the various model types produce causal effect estimates that could vary as a function of the inclusion or omission of these potential confounds.

ables shown earlier in Table 2.1 that were identified in the literature as potential confounds). The extent to which the model fit improves when adding the covariates indicates the extent to which that model type uses the covariates for prediction (i.e., the extent to which the model residuals are associated with the covariate when the variable is omitted). Thus, this change in fit also indicates the extent that the model's causal effect estimates would be sensitive to omitting these covariates.

Table 3.5 presents the model fits for each model type, both when including and when omitting all available covariates. The model fit index is the 50-fold cross-validated error of prediction expressed in the normal units of the negative binomial loss function.[5] All models were run as negative binomial, although linear models produce substantively identical results. The *change in fit* column in Table 3.5 assesses the extent to which the effect estimates from each model may be sensitive to omitting these covariates; a zero change in fit indicates that the

Table 3.5
Effect of Adding Covariates on Model Fit (Cross-Validated Error), by Model Type

Model	Omitting Covariates	Including Covariates	Change in fit
Base model (time-fixed effects)	2,667	907	1,760
+ autoregressive effect	105	105	0
+ state-fixed effects	440	277	163
+ autoregressive effect and state-fixed effects	111	105	6
+ state-fixed effects and state trends	171	128	42

NOTES: Results are based on a negative binomial regression. The error of prediction from 50-fold cross-validation is quantified as the model deviance using the standard loss function for negative binomial regression, with zero representing perfect prediction of the number of firearm deaths in every state and year.

---

[5] This fit index is very similar to the more common Akaike information criterion (AIC) (Akaike, 1974) fit index. The AIC is asymptotically equivalent to cross-validated error when the model likelihood function is correct. However, some of the tested models use a likelihood function that incorrectly assumes independence of observations within state. This would cause the AIC to overestimate the quality of the fit in those models.

model produces residuals that were independent of the covariates even when the covariates were omitted from the model (i.e., the covariates are not needed for prediction), and larger values indicate increasing sensitivity of the estimates to the inclusion of these covariates.

Table 3.5 shows that the base model without either state-fixed effects or autoregressive effects was highly sensitive to covariates. Including covariates in this type of model eliminated 66 percent of the error of prediction relative to the model without covariates. These covariates were highly associated with the rate of firearm deaths across states and years, even after controlling for the national time trend. In contrast, including covariates in the autoregressive model had no measurable effect on the error of prediction; the association of the covariates on the outcome was fully captured by controlling for the total firearm deaths in the prior year, even when the covariates themselves were omitted from that model. Adding state-fixed effects to the base model did provide considerable robustness against omitted covariates relative to the performance of the base model. And adding state-specific trends to this model further improved its robustness to omitted covariates. However, both of these models were still more sensitive to omitted covariates than the autoregressive model.

Somewhat surprisingly, adding state-fixed effects to the autoregressive model made the model more sensitive to omitting the covariates, although the difference is trivial. This occurred because adding the state effect to the autoregressive model without covariates actually resulted in more error of prediction (error of 111 versus 105). In other words, adding 49 parameters to the model promoted overfitting without improved explanation of variance, resulting in a worse-fitting model.

Overall, these results suggest that researchers using models without either autoregressive effects or state-fixed effects should be concerned about the extent to which their findings are robust with respect to omitted covariates. In contrast, the effect estimates from the autoregressive models are highly insensitive to the inclusion or exclusion of covariates, and that robustness is not improved by also adding state-fixed effects to the autoregressive model. This finding—coupled with the earlier findings that adding fixed effects to an autoregressive model increased type 1 error, decreased the rate of correct rejections, and increased magnitude bias—suggests that fixed effects should not be added to the autoregressive models of firearm deaths.

Another consideration in model selection for causal inference in longitudinal data is the extent to which the model is resistant to artifacts caused by regression to the mean. This can be considered to be a type of omitted variable bias where the variable in question is the prior value of the outcome itself. For example, states may choose to enact gun control legislation specifically because their firearm death rate is high. This outcome series shows regression to the mean, in which extremely high or low rates of firearm deaths are likely to be followed by less-extreme rates in the subsequent years. Thus, if the passage of the law is predicated on an unusually high rate of gun deaths, the state may be expected to show improvement over time even if the law has no true causal effect.

The autoregressive models have a high degree of resistance to artifacts caused by regression to the mean. This is because they directly condition on the prior value on the outcome; the model does not assume that expected change is independent of the pretreatment value (Barnett, Van Der Pols, and Dobson, 2005). In contrast, difference-in-differences models (e.g., models including year and state-fixed effects) are susceptible to these artifacts whenever the treated and untreated units (e.g., states) show converging trends over time (e.g., trends with larger differences in their means during the pre-period than in the post-period (Angrist and Pischke, 2009). Additional analyses may be performed to rule out the possibility of artifacts because of regression to the mean in such a model, for example, by demonstrating that the treated and untreated states had similar means in the pre-law period. However, the effect is not estimated in a manner that accounts for the extent of mean reversion that is shown in the data. Similarly, a first-differences model could be used instead of an autoregressive model to investigate a law's effect. Such a model differs from an autoregressive model only in that a first-differences model assumes there is no regression to the mean, while an autoregressive model estimates the extent to which observations regress to the mean over time and controls for that change. In situations in which the probability of passing the law may be influenced by the level of firearm deaths, the first-differences approach may result in artifacts caused by regression to the mean (Rubin, 1977).

A third consideration when selecting a model is the extent to which the findings can be used to demonstrate temporal precedence—that is, the effect requires that the law was implemented prior to the shift in death rates in the implementing states. Temporal precedence is one of the key criteria for inferring causation (Hume, [1748] 2004; Mill, 1843), and the ability to investigate precedence is one of the primary reasons researchers turn to longitudinal data to investigate causation. However, not all models are equally good at demonstrating precedence.

Models that do not control for either autoregressive effects or state-fixed effects (such as the GEE models used in the simulations) have causal effects that are indicated both by differences across states and by differences within a state over time. Thus, if states with persistently high firearm death rates are more likely to implement a given law, such a model is likely to show a positive effect of the law on death rates, even if there is no change in rates over time either in the states that implemented the law or in those that did not. In spite of the fact that these models are estimated on longitudinal data, this analysis does not demonstrate that the assumed cause precedes the effect.

Including the state- and year-fixed effects to create a difference-in-differences model improves the ability of the model to demonstrate temporal precedence. Effects are now indicated solely through changes from the pre-law mean to the post-law mean in the treated relative to control states. However, in a long time series, there may be substantial variability in the outcome within both the pre-law period and the post-law period (e.g., a law that was implemented in year ten of a 20-year time series and that shows a difference-in-differences effect of decreasing the firearm death rate by one per 100,000 people). Such a difference in pre-post means could occur with several distinct temporal trajectories:

- The death rate could have shown a persistent relative decrease for implementing states starting in year ten by one death per 100,000 people.

- The death rate could have showed a persistent relative decrease for implementing states in year 15 by two per 100,000 people.
- The death rate could have showed a persistent relative decrease for implementing states in year five by two per 100,000 people.

Each of these three scenarios would show decreases in the relative death rates in implementing states by one per 100,000 in the pre- versus post-period. These all yield the same difference-in-differences effect estimate. However, in the third scenario, the model explains a shift in rates that occurs in year five of the series as being caused by a law that was not passed until five years later. Thus, while difference-in-differences models do indicate the causal effect through a shift in the relative means from the pre-law to the post-law period, this does not always ensure that the data would show a change in the relative death rate after the law was implemented were the data to be analyzed in a more fine-grained temporal scale. While it is possible to assess this threat to the validity by investigating the parallel trends assumption within the data, there is no generally accepted solution when the trends between implementing and nonimplementing states diverge prior to implementation (see, for example, Angrist and Pischke, 2008).

In contrast, autoregressive models with *change coded* effects are indicated by the association between year-over-year changes in the death rate with the year-over-year changes in the law. This can be seen earlier in Table 2.2, which provided an example of change coding. When testing for an instant effect, the effect is indicated entirely by whether the death rate is higher or lower in the first year after implementation relative to what was expected based on the prior year's death rate, that year's fixed effects, and the covariates. Similarly, with a five-year phase-in period, the effect is indicated only by changes in the death rates over the five-year period during which the law's effect was phasing in. Thus, this type of model shows an effect only when there is a year-over-year change in the death rate in the years immediately after implementation.

While this temporal specificity of the autoregressive *change coding* model is a benefit from the perspective of drawing causal inferences, it also presents a practical challenge. In a typical difference-in-differences model estimated within a moderately long time series, there is little penalty if the exact timing of the law's implementation is mis-specified. For example, in a 30-year time series, the difference between the pre- and post-implementation means will be approximately the same if the implementation date shifts by a year; this only moves one observation out of 30 from the pre- to the post-period. Using the autoregressive change coding model, however, shifting the date by one year could yield an entirely different and unrelated effect. Because this model makes full use of the temporal resolution of the outcome measure, it is very sensitive to specifying the correct timing of the law's effects. In practical applications in which implementation date or the length of the phase-in period is not precisely known, these models may benefit from using a more-flexible function than a single spline to allow for the possibility that the true phase-in period is somewhat longer or shorter than assumed.

Finally, researchers generally prefer likelihood functions (i.e., the model and link-function, along with any assumptions about the error distributions) that do not require postestimation corrections to the SEs (e.g., cluster adjustments) to compensate for mis-specification (Freedman, 2006). Using an effect estimate that requires such a correction presents limitations in the range of analyses that could be performed and may result in other problems even when they do improve type 1 error. Specifically, these adjustments are used to correct Wald tests of significance; however, we know of no generally accepted method to apply a similar correction to likelihood ratio tests (see Yuan and Bentler, 2000, for an attempt to extend Huber corrections to likelihood ratio tests). However, likelihood ratio tests are often preferred for certain types of hypothesis tests, including any tests involving random effects or joint tests of model parameters. Similarly, the need for a clustering correction when using a difference-in-differences model may preclude using Bayesian methods to estimate the effects or Bayesian methods of hypothesis testing. In short, the need for these corrections generally restricts the options available to the statistical analyst, ruling out many standard procedures. For this reason, it is preferable to use one of the autoregressive models that accurately characterizes the uncertainty in the estimates without any postestimation corrections.

A related problem occurs because almost all common model fit indices (e.g., Akaike's information criterion or Bayesian information criteria) are based on the model likelihood and are closely related to likelihood ratio tests. This may result in the researcher underestimating problems with his or her models because the fit indices assume a substantially inflated number of independent observations in the data. Some of the estimated models have a large number of parameters (as many as 150) and may be at risk of being overfit. However, the standard tools for investigating this problem cannot be trusted when a cluster adjustment is required—that is, when the model likelihood is incorrect (Burnham and Anderson, 2002).

Finally, using these adjustments applied after model estimation could result in both estimation issues within the model and interpretation problems for researchers. In many models, changing the type of error distribution or its variance should affect the point estimates themselves, although this will not occur for these methods of adjustment (Freedman, 2006). The need for such corrections may also represent more-fundamental problems with the model, which could lead to effects being expressed in incorrect units or forms. This may make it difficult to generalize the effect outside of the sample in which it was estimated or result in predicted values that are impossible (Freedman, 2006).

When possible, it is preferable to incorporate the important regular features of the data into the likelihood function itself rather than to rely on postestimation adjustments to SEs. When investigating a law that has been passed in 35 or more states, the models without autoregressive effects perform quite similarly to the autoregressive models on type 1 error, correct rejection rate, and bias. Those models, however, always require a postestimation adjustment to the SEs because their likelihood function ignores the high correlation between temporally adjacent observations within a state. Even in situations in which a large number of states implemented the law, it may still be preferable to use an autoregressive model that incorporates this feature of the data into the model itself.

CHAPTER FOUR

Discussion

This study identified one method of estimating the causal effect of state laws on firearm death rates that was preferable to all of the others we considered across the range of conditions included in the simulation. The best model was a negative binomial autoregressive model that used change coding of the state laws and did not include state-fixed or random effects or any adjustments to the SEs. This model was slightly conservative with respect to type 1 error, averaging 3-percent false positives rather than the nominal 5 percent. It produced some of the lowest variance estimates, resulting in the highest rate of correct rejections when there was a true effect of the law. It demonstrated low directional and magnitude bias in the estimated effects and displayed very low bias when 15 or more states implemented the law. In addition, the model showed other desirable features, including producing effect estimates that were the most robust to omitted covariates and incorporating protections against artifacts caused by regression to the mean that could occur when the implementation of the law is associated with the preexisting firearm death rate. The model also did the best job of ensuring that the implementation of the law preceded the change in firearm death rates that is the assumed causal effect of the law. Finally, the model also did not require any postestimation adjustment to the modeled SEs.

In contrast to the relatively good performance of the preferred model, several other common methods showed serious problems when used to estimate the effects of gun laws on state-by-year firearm death rates. Relative to the preferred model, all models that eliminated the autoregressive path resulted in highly biased SEs and high rates of false positives. Some relatively common model specifications that have appeared in this literature showed type 1 error rates of 50 percent or more, including several popular log-linear models, some weighted linear models, and some negative binomial models. This problem is improved somewhat with the addition of a clustering adjustment or use of GEE methods; however, these corrections worked only when a large number of states implemented the law (replicating Bertrand, Duflo, and Mullainathan, 2004), and, even in the best case, the type 1 error when not including an autoregressive effect was often at least twice the nominal rate of 5 percent.

Adding state-fixed or random effects to the preferred model does not appear to improve model performance. These changes generally increased false positives when the null was true and decreased correct rejections when the null was false. They also resulted in slight underestimates of the magnitude of the true effect size. Somewhat surprisingly, we found no evidence that adding state-fixed effects to the autoregressive model improved robustness to omitted variable biases.

One of the most novel features investigated in this study was the use of *change coding* in autoregressive models. This type of variable coding is typically used with first-differences models, which are closely related to autoregressive models when the autoregressive coefficient is near one. However, we are aware of no other studies that have employed this type of variable coding with autoregressive models. Relative to standard *effect coding*, the autoregressive models using *change coding* showed substantially less bias in the effect magnitude estimates. The *effect coded* autoregressive models estimated effects as small as 13 percent of the true effect magnitude (i.e., a bias equal to 87 percent of the true effect size). Correspondingly, the models had considerably less power to detect a true effect. In the best-case scenario, the preferred model correctly rejected the null hypothesis 50 percent of the time, while the version using *effect coding* correctly rejected the null hypothesis 15 percent of the time in the same condition.

Concerns About Low Power

Although the study was successful in identifying statistical methods that are best for estimating the effect of state laws on firearm deaths, the findings also highlighted some substantial challenges to drawing such inferences. Perhaps the largest challenge to the field is the extremely low power shown to detect a meaningfully large effect of gun laws on firearm deaths.

This study revealed low rates of correct rejections of the null hypothesis even under ideal conditions that exaggerate the power that would be available when investigating real-world laws. In particular, we always tested for the exact phase-in period of the true effect of the law. However, when working with real laws, there may be substantial uncertainty about the amount of time before the full effect of the law will be manifest in the data. While it is possible to deal with this uncertainty in the analysis, it will inevitably either increase the variance of the estimate (if a flexible function for a range of possible phase-in periods is used) or cause an underestimation of the true effect (if a single phase-in period that is not exactly correct is selected). Both of these will reduce the likelihood of correctly rejecting the null hypothesis. The other major reason that our study overestimates power is that in the simulation, the implementation of laws was independent from all covariates and the preimplementation rate of firearm deaths. Actual gun laws, however, are often highly associated with state characteristics. Such associations necessarily increase the variance of the effect estimates in analyses that control for those characteristics and subsequently reduce the probability of correctly detecting when there is a true effect of the law.

Some may argue that our current estimates of statistical power are low because we chose to simulate an effect size that was too small to have a truly meaningful effect or that most actual firearm laws should be expected to have substantially larger effects than examined here. Statistical power would obviously improve for all models if simulated with a larger effect size, and we believe that policymakers do and should care about gun laws that are on the order of increasing or decreasing the total number of firearm deaths by 1,000 per year. In our survey of a diverse sample of gun policy experts (Morral, Schell, and Tankard, 2018), we found that, when an expert believed a policy would increase suicide and homicide by 3 percent, the expert also believed the policy should not be implemented; when the expert believed the policy would decrease these outcomes by 3 percent, they strongly supported implementation. Similarly, other domains in which public policy could affect 1,000 deaths per year are often treated as serious problems or solutions. For example, regulations shifting the minimum legal drinking age from 18 to 21 are estimated by the U.S. National Highway Traffic Safety Administration to have caused a reduction in traffic fatalities of about 826 lives per year (U.S. Department of Transportation, National Highway Traffic Safety Administration, 2009). Similarly, the annual coalition deaths in Operation Iraqi Freedom never exceeded 1,000 per year but were seen as a serious policy concern. Annual effects this large add up to an enormous loss (or savings) of life when considered over a decade or a generation.

It would be difficult to justify an expectation that a given state gun policy has a substantially larger effect on firearm deaths than what we have modeled. Policies that prevent large proportions of the population from possessing firearms have been ruled unconstitutional (see, for example, *District of Columbia v Heller*), and most firearm policy changes are highly targeted to specific types of individuals or situations. For example, our review of the existing literature suggests that child-access prevention laws have some of the strongest empirical evidence of effectiveness (RAND Corporation, undated). However, these laws are targeted at gun owners living with minors who do not currently store their firearms safely, with the stated goal of reducing child use of firearms. However, according to the CDC's Fatal Injury Reports, there were 1,296 firearm suicides among people ages 20 or younger and 489 unintentional firearm deaths among youths in 2015 (CDC, 2018). Only a proportion of these deaths could realistically be prevented by increasing liability for unsafe firearm storage. Thus, it appears plausible to expect that even one of the most widely supported state firearm policies will have an effect on firearm deaths that is fewer than 1,000 deaths per year. While there may be specific policies for which one could realistically expect a decrease in deaths by greater than 3 percent per year, this percentage is nevertheless a reasonable effect size for many commonly discussed gun policies and is large enough for policymakers, the public, and gun policy experts to care about.

The finding that there is typically very low power (e.g., often less than a 15-percent chance of correctly rejecting the null hypothesis with a standard difference-in-differences model) may come as a surprise to some. There are a large number of published papers in this literature, most of which report many $p < 0.05$ effects. The current simulations suggest that a substantial reason for this apparent paradox is that almost all of the studies in the existing literature have statistical methods that underestimated the uncertainty in their effects, leading to inflated claims of statistical significance. Comparing the findings in Table 3.1 to the methods used in the existing literature, it appears that the true likelihood of a false positive may be closer to one in six across these models than the one-in-20 rate that is claimed. This problem is exacerbated by a tendency to run a single conceptual analysis several different ways (e.g., effects estimated with different sets of covariates; effects estimated within each racial, gender, or age group; effects estimated within individual states). When presenting 30 or more significance tests, each of which may have a one-in-six chance of producing a false positive, it is possible to have an article with many significant effects even when the null hypothesis is true.

Operating with such low statistical power may represent a challenge to the idea that empirical research can effectively guide firearm policy. The key problem is that, even when a policy is truly effective at reducing deaths (or truly harmful and causing deaths), it will be rare that research will find the effect to be statistically significant at a true $p < 0.05$. Even after the policy has been implemented within 25 states and even after a decade of follow-up data have been collected, we should not expect to find a statistically significant result even if the policy in question actually resulted in 5,000 excess deaths over that period within the implementing states. Unlike many scientific domains, there is no obvious way to increase power through additional data collection. This low power occurs even when there is a data set that includes a full census of firearm deaths for the entire country for the last 36 years. There are no additional data.

When working in such a low statistical power environment, there are statistical problems that will plague the field even when significant results are found. Such a field will suffer from three well-documented problems. First, a large fraction of significant results will be spurious (false positives) rather than correct rejections. When the power to detect the true effect is only 10 percent or 20 percent, it requires that, for every significant published result, many additional statistical tests must have been run. Each of these tests has at least a 5-percent chance of creating a false positive when the null is true. The consequence is that the published literature based on the corpus of significant results will necessarily contain a high fraction of findings that are spurious. The second problem is related to the first and is more damaging: A nontrivial fraction of significant results are likely to be in the wrong direction relative to the true effect. In the limit, when statistical power goes to α (e.g., $p < 0.05$), half of all significant effects are in the opposite direction as the true effect. Gelman and Tuerlinckx (2000) have referred to this as "type S" error for sign error.

In our simulations, we documented type S error performance. All of the models had poor type S error in the three-state condition. For example, on 18 percent of the occasions in which the null hypothesis was rejected in the three-state, five-year phase-in condition using our preferred specification, the effect was in the wrong direction relative to the true effect. However, almost all other models performed even worse in this same condition, with type S error rates as high as 37 percent. In contrast, the preferred model demonstrated type S error rates well below 1 percent in the 35-state conditions. This low rate of type S errors was also observed for other model specifications within any conditions in which they produced correct rejection rates above 0.20.

The third interpretational problem that occurs when operating with low statistical power is related to the fact that only a relatively large effect estimate will ever be found to be significant. This results in the significant effect sizes being dramatically unrepresentative of the true effect size (Gelman and Carlin, 2014). Indeed, within our simulations, essentially all significant effects were of a greater magnitude than the actual effect size; samples that yielded an effect that was actually representative of the true effect were almost never significant. Thus, even when the significant effects were not spurious, they were some-times in the incorrect direction and were highly misleading about the effect size.

It is clear that having low statistical power is a problem not only because it makes it less likely to get significant results but also because it presents severe limitations on the ability to interpret the few "sig-nificant" effects that are found (Button et al., 2013; Cohen, 1988). Our uncomfortable conclusion is that, when working in a low-power statistical environment, the standard procedures based on exclusively interpreting effects that are statistically significant is not helpful for guiding policy. The literature that results from these methods is likely to have a high proportion of spurious effects, contradictory findings, and exaggerated claims.

One strategy to address these problems would be for researchers to evaluate the effects of gun policy using Bayesian statistical methods, which describe the range of possible true effects that are consistent with the available data (given the model and researcher-specified prior pos-sibility distributions). This could avoid most of the problems resulting from relying on statistical significance as an indicator of importance within low-power statistical situations (see, for example, Gelman and Tuerlinckx, 2000).

We are aware of the irony that a study that is designed to assess the quality of the statistical inferences from a range of methods ends up recommending that we not make such inferences in the way we inves-tigated. However, the results of the simulations also have clear implica-tions for Bayesian analyses. The investigation into type 1 error could also be interpreted as an investigation into which model accurately esti-mates the variance of the posterior distribution, while the investigation into correct rejections could be seen as a method to identify the mini-mum variance estimator. These desirable properties of our preferred model relative to the alternatives are as useful in Bayesian estimation as in more-common frequentists methods.

Moving from frequentist hypothesis testing to Bayesian effect estimation could mitigate some of the dangers of working with lim-ited data. However, it does not change the fact that, at least in those situations with correct rejection rates less than 10 percent, the data do not provide much useful information about the true effect size or direction. This suggests that there is little possible value of analyzing the effects of state laws until they have been implemented in three or more states—even in a Bayesian framework. Such an analysis is likely to return an estimated posterior distribution of the effect that is functionally equivalent to whatever prior distribution was specified by the researcher. In contrast, hypothesis testing using frequentist methods will still reject the null for the most extreme 5 percent of estimates, regardless of how little information about the effect is contained in the data. Those who wish to continue to use frequentist hypothesis testing should restrict their analysis to situations in which they can demonstrate, at a minimum, greater than 20-percent statistical power to detect a meaningful effect—and preferably greater than 50 percent (Gelman and Carlin, 2014). This will likely require only testing for significant effects of state laws after approximately 20 or more states have implemented a given law and ensures that the modeling approach selected has well-calibrated type 1 error rates. In practice, this may require demonstrating through such simulations as those described in this report that show that the selected model performs as expected with the data being modeled.

Common Adjustments to Standard Errors Often Were Insufficient

Although the primary purpose of the study was to identify the best model for a specific purpose and data set, there are several broader methodological recommendations and observations from the findings that may apply to other data sets. One somewhat surprising finding was the extent to which common "corrections" designed to improve SEs could actually damage statistical inference.

The ubiquitous sandwich-estimated "robust" SEs, which are designed to be robust in the presence of violations of distributional assumptions, almost always resulted in worse type 1 error performance. Not only did these problems with the correction occur with the negative binomial models for which most researchers would probably not to apply such a correction, but they also occurred when analyzing the rate outcome with a linear model. Such corrections are common when using linear models with nonlinear outcomes, but it appears they should be used very cautiously. While everyone would like their inferences to be "robust" to violated assumptions, this correction could have a substantial penalty in some situations. In particular, researchers should be most concerned when the robustness correction results in smaller SEs than the modeled SEs.

The clustering adjustments (either using GEE estimation or a standard cluster adjustment for autoregressive data structure) were also somewhat problematic within the simulations relative to including autoregressive effects directly within the model. When these corrections were used with the autoregressive models, these typically resulted in worse statistical inferences. This appears to be a case in which "belt and suspenders" is actually more dangerous than just the "belt." When this correction was used with the nonautoregressive models, it generally improved inferences. However, the correction was often substantially insufficient, particularly when effects were estimated within a small number of clustering units. Given the limited number of states in the United States, this may present a problem for most research conducted at the state level. There has been some recent theoretical work trying to outline the type of data for which a clustering adjustment should be used (Abadie et al., 2017). However, this work does not discuss the risks of using this adjustment or provide detailed practical guidance on how to determine when the adjustment has made the SEs less accurate.

Log Transformation of Rate Outcomes Resulted in Inference Errors

Similarly, it is standard within some disciplines to apply a log transformations to a rate or count outcome prior to analysis with a linear model. While it is clear that the assumptions of a standard linear model are likely to be violated in untransformed rate data, particularly in data sets with observations at or near the zero bound,[1] it is not obvious that applying a log transformation will result in a model whose assumptions are better met. In the current data, this transformation solved none of the inferential problems with the linear model and actually made things slightly worse. When such transformations are used, it would be best if researchers provided empirical justification within the data set for the specific transformation chosen. Researchers should also justify preferences for using a log-transformed outcome over the more general approach of using a generalized linear model with a log-link function for such data.

Limitations

This study focused exclusively on state-level firearm deaths as the outcome of interest. It is likely that the results will not generalize to other types of outcomes (e.g., other crime data, death rates within narrow demographic groups, death rates for counties) if those outcomes do not share the same key data features. For example, we expect that linear models will perform worse for outcomes that are closer to the zero bound (e.g., analyses of firearm homicides) relative to their performance with total firearm deaths. Perhaps most importantly, we expect the change-coding autoregressive model to perform more poorly for data with lower serial autocorrelation. It is beyond the scope of this study to identify the level of autocorrelation below which our preferred model is no longer the most appropriate option or to identify methods that are well optimized in all situations. Given the ubiquity of difference-in-differences analyses applied to autoregressive sequences within the fields of policy evaluation and economics, this appears to be an area ripe for additional research.

This study was also limited due to the finite range of policy features and statistical methods that we explored. The results may have

---

[1]   Unfortunately, an actual log transformation of the outcome cannot be applied when there are values of zero in the data. Thus, it may not be useful in exactly the situation in which the linear model is most likely to be inappropriate.

been somewhat different if we had, for example, looked at the performance with laws implemented in all 50 states with a ten-year phase-in or if we had simulated laws whose implementation dates were closely bunched. We also did not investigate situations in which the probability of having the law was associated with covariates or unmeasured confounders. Those working with specific data features that are not well represented in this study could conduct similar simulations better suited to their situation. We have included the statistical code in a downloadable form to facilitate such extensions.[2]

Similarly, the study did not assess all possible methods for estimating these causal effects. For example, it is possible and often preferable to compute causal effects in longitudinal data using marginal effect estimates rather than directly from model coefficients (see, for example, Robins, Hernan, and Brumback, 2000). Similarly, when the probability of having the law is associated with covariates, it is often preferable to use methods that account for this differential propensity. These methods were not investigated in this study, which did not have such associations, although it is an area for future work. Such work may yet identify methods that are superior to methods we currently prefer on the basis of this simulation study.

There are two relatively common statistical methods that were not included in the full simulation but may be of interest to the field. The first method is to operationalize the effect of policy as a permanent change in the trajectory of the death rate over time. This is closely related to the model we included with state-fixed effects and state-specific linear trends. However, the model used in the literature typically assumes that the trend continues indefinitely, while, in our simulation, the effect of the law asymptotes after a five-year phase-in. While this may seem like a subtle difference, it has substantial implications for both the interpretation of the model and its statistical performance. The primary reason such a model was not included in the simulation is that it is not possible to specify an effect size in such a model that is comparable to the other models. It assumes that the effect size always

---

[2] The statistical code is available on the product page of this report on the RAND Corporation's website.

grows toward positive or negative infinity with sufficient time. Even within our simulation over 36 years, the actual effect size within that period would vary across iterations of the simulation as a function of the random date of law implementation. Although this change in slope specification has been used by several researchers, we do not feel its omission from our simulation is a significant limitation. No researchers have presented a theoretical argument or a proposed data-generation mechanism that justifies the ever-increasing effect size. In addition, there are a range of statistical and interpretational problems with this change in slope model, which we have detailed elsewhere (Appendix A; RAND Corporation, undated). Our view is that the similar model included within the simulation (model with state-fixed effects and linear detrending with a fixed phase-in period of the effect) is a better specification.

The other model specification that was omitted from the study was one in which the causal effect is estimated separately within each of the implementing states; these single-state effect estimates are then aggregated and tested for significance, often using meta-analytic methods. We did include this method in the early versions of the simulations (using the *rmeta* package within R to aggregate single state estimates into an overall effect estimate) but discontinued its use because of severe problems with its estimates. The core issue was that the tests for equality of effects across states were almost always statistically significant, in spite of the fact that the simulated effects were perfectly homogeneous across states. Similarly, the tests of significance for the average effect were also significant almost all the time, even when there was no true effect. Thus, the model with state-by-law effects always performed substantially worse than the corresponding model that directly estimated the average effect across implementing states. Because we did not wish to explore all of the various ways in which these models could be implemented (e.g., state-by-law fixed versus random or various meta-analytic methods for testing for homogeneity or testing the significance of the average effect), we omitted the meta-analytic conditions from the results. Although we did not fully explore this portion of the model space, we suspect that such models are difficult to get correct. For example, there is no way to get correct SEs from a difference-in-differences model fit to autoregressive time-series data with an $N = 1$ effect; the standard cluster adjustments do not work when each effect is estimated on a single case (see Bertrand, Duflo, and Mullainathan, 2004). If the SEs for the individual state effects are routinely a small fraction of the correct value, it is not surprising that one would get high rates of false positives when testing the overall average effects or when testing for equality of effects across states. Currently, several researchers have suggested the need to include such law-by-state interactions on the basis of tests showing significant heterogeneity of effects across states. Our preliminary results suggest that such findings may be spurious and require further methodological investigation before accepting them at face value.

Conclusions

In this report, we showed that most of the statistical methods commonly used to estimate the causal effects of gun laws at the state, county, or city level suffer from important limitations that make inferences from those models prone to error. Almost all models we investigated had SEs that were too small, leading to high false-positive rates. Common adjustments to the SE generally failed to fully correct this problem. All models were found to have insufficient power to detect causal effects that would correspond to an increase or decrease of 1,000 firearm deaths per year nationally, an effect size that we argue is a large enough change to be clearly important. One model, however, performed relatively better than the others we investigated: a negative binomial model of firearm deaths that includes time-fixed effects, an autoregressive lag, and change coding for the law effect. The preferred specification includes no state-fixed effects or SE adjustment.

Our approach to evaluating model performance is not common in the field of gun policy research. Rather than vigorously investigating which set of statistical assumptions are appropriate for the data, researchers more often conduct a large number of sensitivity tests with variations on the model or variations of the SEs. The current results, however, suggest that it is possible to run the model 100 different ways, all of which may produce dramatically underestimated SEs. The number of sensitivity tests performed may provide little information about the quality of the findings. If the sensitivity tests result in a broadly similar pattern of asterisks in the output, the sensitivity tests are very likely to give the authors and the audience false confidence in the robustness of the findings. If the results differ across the sensitivity tests, they provide an opportunity for the researchers' preferences for particular results to play a role in model selection.

We believe a better approach is to select a model based on an investigation into the most appropriate assumption for the data, and then ignore results from all less appropriate models. In our view, the use of sensitivity tests should be restricted to the situations in which it is not possible to determine which method is more appropriate for the data (e.g., whether to include a covariate that could be a confound but could also be endogenous to the causal effect of interest) or when multiple methods have been demonstrated to be equally appropriate. This study demonstrates a novel analytic method to do this type of model selection without necessarily having to test each assumption separately and to then determine which violations are extreme enough to cause concern. The included statistical code could, we hope, facilitate broader adoption of such methods.

In this report, we focused our investigation on selecting the best statistical methods for use in a single data set. In this case, we found very poor statistical performance for almost all of the commonly used models in this field. However, it is possible that substantially different results would be found for alternative outcome variables or data sets. However, we suspect that the problems common models experience in the current data may well generalize to other analytic problems sharing some of the same structural features. Chief among these features appears to be strong autocorrelation in the outcome measure and a relatively limited number of observational units in which the policy of interest was implemented, such as investigations of state-level policies. Further research is needed to identify how many published findings may have been inappropriately identified as statistically significant because of these statistical problems.

Technical Description of Evaluated Models

As noted in the report, two model features were kept constant across all of the models in the simulations: (1) All models include fixed effects for each year of the data series, which effectively controls for national trends in firearm death rates, and (2) all models included the same set of covariates.

Thus, all models were built on a base model of the following form:

$$g(Y_{ts}) = \beta_0 + \beta_1 * f(Z_{ts}, D, C) + \sum_{k=1981}^{2014} \alpha_k 1(t = k) + \sum_{p=1}^{17} \delta_p X_{pts} + \varepsilon_{ts} , (1)$$

where

- $g(.)$ denotes a generic link function
- Y_{ts} denotes the outcome for state s in year t for t = 1981, . . . , 2014
- β_0 represents the model intercept
- β_1 is the effect size estimate for the simulated gun laws
- $f(Z_{ts}, D, C)$ defines the coding of the law as a function of whether the law was in effect in state s and year t (Z_{ts}), whether the law had an instant effect or the effect phased-in linearly over a five-year period (D), and whether the model used change or effect coding of the law (C)
- $1(.)$ denotes an indicator function for the time-fixed effects
- X_{pts} denotes the value of pth covariate (shown in Table 2.1 of the main report).

The function $f(.)$ in equation 1 defines the coding of the law used in the model. *Effect coding* (ε_{ts}) was scaled so that it took on the value of 0 in any year in which the law was not in effect; a 1 in any year in which it was fully in effect; and linearly interpolated, fractional values during any phase in a period specified by D. When creating simulated data under an alternative hypothesis, the true treatment effect was incorporated into the data by multiplying a constant effect by $\varepsilon_{t,s}$ and adding that value to the outcome via the appropriate link function. When using *change coding*, $f(.)$ was defined as the difference in the *effect coding* values between the current year and the prior year for a given state, $\varepsilon_{t,s} - \varepsilon_{t-1,s}$.

In our simulations, we considered two possible link functions: a linear link function and a log-link function. For linear models, we expressed the outcome as the crude firearm death rate per 100,000 people or as the logarithm of that death rate. For log-link models, the outcome was the count of firearm deaths. For log-link models, the logged population of the state was added as an offset to the base model (model 1):

$$+ \ln (P_{ts}).$$

The inclusion of this offset results in the model parameters being interpreted as though the outcome were the firearm death rate rather than the number of deaths. In the case of log-link functions, we evaluated the negative binomial, Poisson, and quasi-Poisson models in our simulation, but the negative binomial model always outperformed the other two. For the sake of simplicity, we presented the results for only the negative binomial models in the report.

In our autoregressive models, we control for lagged effects of the outcome by adding lagged values of the outcome into the right-hand side of model 1:

$$+ \beta_2 * \ln (Y_{t-1,s}/P_{t-1,s})$$ when the model uses a log-link.

$$+ \beta_2 * Y_{t-1,s}$$ when the model uses a linear link.

In models that included state-fixed effects, we add to model 1

$$\sum\nolimits_{m=2}^{50} \rho_m 1\, (s = state\ m)_.$$

For models that include state random effects, we revise this term to be

$$\sum\nolimits_{m=1}^{50} \rho_m_.$$

where ρ_m for $m = 1, \ldots, 50$ is assumed to have a normal distribution with mean vector μ and variance-covariance matrix Σ.

Code for our models is provided in the public use code and data set that accompanies this report.

Standard Error Correction Factors

Table B.1 shows the correction factors for all models.

Table B.1
Standard Error Correction Factors for Each Model, by Number of Implementing States and Length of Phase-in Period

Model Type	Autoregression Effect	State Effect	SE Adjustment	Instant Phase-in (No. of Years)			Five Year Phase-in (No. of Years)			Average	Worst
				3	15	35	3	15	35		
Negative binomial	Change	None	None	0.97	0.96	0.97	0.89	0.88	0.84	0.92	0.84*
Negative binomial	Change	None	Cluster	2.17	1.17	1.07	1.80	1.14	1.06	1.40	2.17
Negative binomial	Effect	None	None	1.24	1.18	1.15	1.23	1.19	1.18	1.19	1.24*
Negative binomial	Effect	None	Cluster	1.68	1.25	1.23	1.65	1.25	1.24	1.38	1.68
Negative binomial	Change	Fixed	None	1.03	1.02	1.02	1.20	1.27	1.27	1.13	1.27*
Negative binomial	Change	Fixed	Cluster	2.07	1.16	1.07	1.71	1.19	1.17	1.40	2.07
Negative binomial	Effect	Fixed	None	1.85	1.80	1.64	1.99	1.91	1.70	1.82	1.99
Negative binomial	Effect	Fixed	Cluster	1.61	1.25	1.25	1.59	1.28	1.23	1.37	1.61*
Negative binomial	None	Fixed	None	3.35	3.16	2.85	3.55	3.31	3.08	3.22	3.55
Negative binomial	None	Fixed	Cluster	1.58	1.12	1.09	1.58	1.13	1.09	1.26	1.58
Negative binomial	None	Fixed and trend	None	2.31	2.35	2.31	2.52	2.59	2.55	2.44	2.59
Negative binomial	None	Fixed and trend	Cluster	1.94	1.22	1.12	1.99	1.25	1.14	1.44	1.99*
Log linear–weighted	None	Fixed	None	5.27	5.19	4.68	5.54	5.46	5.01	5.19	5.54

Table B.1—Continued

Model Type	Autoregression Effect	State Effect	SE Adjustment	Instant Phase-in (No. of Years)			Five Year Phase-in (No. of Years)				
				3	15	35	3	15	35	Average	Worst
Log linear-weighted	None	Fixed	Huber	3.85	3.93	3.76	4.28	4.16	4.00	4.00	4.28
Log linear-weighted	None	Fixed	Cluster	1.89	1.36	1.36	1.94	1.36	1.35	1.54	1.94*
Log linear-weighted	None	Fixed	Both	3.74	3.82	3.65	4.15	4.04	3.88	3.88	4.15
Linear-weighted	Change	None	None	1.15	1.17	1.20	1.15	1.25	1.20	1.18	1.25*
Linear-weighted	Change	None	Huber	1.89	1.19	1.12	1.17	1.13	1.07	1.26	1.89
Linear-weighted	Change	None	Cluster	2.35	1.26	1.16	1.93	1.30	1.18	1.53	2.35
Linear-weighted	Change	None	Both	1.86	1.17	1.10	1.15	1.12	1.06	1.24	1.86
Linear-weighted	Effect	None	None	1.39	1.39	1.37	1.38	1.37	1.36	1.38	1.39
Linear-weighted	Effect	None	Huber	1.32	1.37	1.30	1.38	1.38	1.34	1.35	1.38
Linear-weighted	Effect	None	Cluster	1.87	1.51	1.42	1.89	1.48	1.44	1.60	1.89
Linear-weighted	Effect	None	Both	1.30	1.35	1.28	1.36	1.36	1.32	1.33	1.36*
Linear-weighted	Change	Fixed	None	1.23	1.25	1.28	1.37	1.63	1.59	1.39	1.63*

Table B.1—Continued

Model Type	Autoregression Effect	State Effect	SE Adjustment	Instant Phase-in (No. of Years)			Five Year Phase-in (No. of Years)			Average	Worst
				3	15	35	3	15	35		
Linear–weighted	Change	Fixed	Huber	1.86	1.28	1.18	1.39	1.44	1.44	1.43	1.86
Linear–weighted	Change	Fixed	Cluster	2.32	1.29	1.19	1.88	1.32	1.29	1.55	2.32
Linear–weighted	Change	Fixed	Both	1.80	1.24	1.14	1.35	1.40	1.40	1.39	1.80
Linear–weighted	Effect	Fixed	None	2.07	1.96	1.90	2.12	2.02	1.95	2.00	2.12
Linear–weighted	Effect	Fixed	Huber	1.80	1.81	1.73	1.93	1.90	1.79	1.82	1.93
Linear–weighted	Effect	Fixed	Cluster	1.88	1.48	1.40	1.86	1.49	1.40	1.58	1.88
Linear–weighted	Effect	Fixed	Both	1.74	1.75	1.68	1.87	1.84	1.74	1.77	1.87*
Linear–weighted	Change	Random	None	1.16	1.16	1.20	1.14	1.25	1.22	1.19	1.25*
Linear–weighted	Effect	Random	None	1.22	1.24	1.20	1.21	1.23	1.22	1.22	1.24*
Linear–weighted	None	None	GEE	2.19	1.29	1.18	2.01	1.31	1.18	1.53	2.19*
Linear–weighted	None	Fixed	None	4.57	4.31	4.17	4.79	4.58	4.37	4.46	4.79
Linear–weighted	None	Fixed	Huber	3.77	3.64	3.39	4.09	3.89	3.62	3.73	4.09
Linear–weighted	None	Fixed	Cluster	1.94	1.44	1.38	1.95	1.44	1.36	1.59	1.95*
Linear–weighted	None	Fixed	Both	3.66	3.54	3.29	3.97	3.78	3.51	3.62	3.97

Table B.1—Continued

Model Type	Autoregression Effect	State Effect	SE Adjustment	Instant Phase-in (No. of Years)			Five Year Phase-in (No. of Years)			Average	Worst
				3	15	35	3	15	35		
Linear–weighted	None	Fixed and trend	None	2.82	2.98	2.97	3.08	3.30	3.24	3.07	3.30
Linear–weighted	None	Fixed and trend	Huber	2.49	2.58	2.56	2.85	2.94	2.89	2.72	2.94
Linear–weighted	None	Fixed and trend	Cluster	2.09	1.45	1.32	2.13	1.45	1.32	1.63	2.13*
Linear–weighted	None	Fixed and trend	Both	2.39	2.47	2.45	2.73	2.82	2.77	2.60	2.82
Linear–unweighted	Change	None	None	0.95	0.95	0.95	0.76	0.75	0.70	0.85	0.70*
Linear–unweighted	Change	None	Huber	1.49	1.01	0.96	0.94	0.81	0.72	0.99	1.49
Linear–unweighted	Change	None	Cluster	1.89	1.11	1.04	1.56	1.10	1.02	1.29	1.89
Linear–unweighted	Change	None	Both	1.47	0.99	0.95	0.92	0.79	0.71	0.97	1.47
Linear–unweighted	Effect	None	None	1.04	1.01	1.01	1.03	1.00	0.99	1.01	1.04*
Linear–unweighted	Effect	None	Huber	1.25	1.13	1.07	1.26	1.13	1.07	1.15	1.26
Linear–unweighted	Effect	None	Cluster	1.41	1.17	1.14	1.41	1.18	1.15	1.24	1.41
Linear–unweighted	Effect	None	Both	1.23	1.11	1.05	1.24	1.11	1.05	1.13	1.24
Linear–unweighted	Change	Fixed	None	0.99	0.99	0.98	1.06	1.01	1.02	1.01	1.06*
Linear–unweighted	Change	Fixed	Huber	1.51	1.11	1.03	1.26	1.09	1.08	1.18	1.51

Table B.1—Continued

Model Type	Autoregression Effect	State Effect	SE Adjustment	Instant Phase-in (No. of Years)			Five Year Phase-in (No. of Years)			Average	Worst
				3	15	35	3	15	35		
Linear–unweighted	Change	Fixed	Cluster	1.86	1.12	1.03	1.64	1.09	1.05	1.30	1.86
Linear–unweighted	Change	Fixed	Both	1.47	1.08	1.00	1.23	1.06	1.05	1.14	1.47
Linear–unweighted	Effect	Fixed	None	1.45	1.39	1.32	1.50	1.46	1.37	1.41	1.50
Linear–unweighted	Effect	Fixed	Huber	1.62	1.50	1.37	1.68	1.56	1.41	1.52	1.68
Linear–unweighted	Effect	Fixed	Cluster	1.47	1.13	1.07	1.48	1.16	1.06	1.23	1.48*
Linear–unweighted	Effect	Fixed	Both	1.57	1.45	1.32	1.63	1.51	1.37	1.48	1.63
Linear–unweighted	Change	Random	None	0.97	0.97	0.96	0.95	0.92	0.93	0.95	0.92*
Linear–unweighted	Effect	Random	None	1.26	1.22	1.17	1.30	1.28	1.20	1.24	1.30*
Linear–unweighted	None	None	GEE	1.82	1.12	1.07	1.77	1.11	1.03	1.32	1.82*
Linear–unweighted	None	Fixed	None	2.67	2.59	2.36	2.76	2.70	2.47	2.59	2.76
Linear–unweighted	None	Fixed	Huber	2.87	2.68	2.43	2.99	2.81	2.56	2.73	2.99
Linear–unweighted	None	Fixed	Cluster	1.58	1.18	1.09	1.60	1.18	1.08	1.28	1.60*
Linear–unweighted	None	Fixed	Both	2.79	2.61	2.36	2.91	2.73	2.49	2.65	2.91
Linear–unweighted	None	Fixed and trend	None	2.01	1.99	1.95	2.09	2.14	2.11	2.05	2.14

Table B.1—Continued

Model Type	Autoregression Effect	State Effect	SE Adjustment	Instant Phase-in (No. of Years)			Five Year Phase-in (No. of Years)			Average	Worst
				3	15	35	3	15	35		
Linear–unweighted	None	Fixed and trend	Huber	2.01	1.99	1.97	2.22	2.21	2.16	2.09	2.22
Linear–unweighted	None	Fixed and trend	Cluster	1.70	1.13	1.07	1.68	1.15	1.07	1.30	1.70*
Linear–unweighted	None	Fixed and trend	Both	1.92	1.91	1.88	2.13	2.11	2.07	2.00	2.13

NOTES: All tests conducted with $\alpha = 0.05$. *Average* (in the header row) refers to the average correction factor over the six simulation conditions for each model. *Worst* refers to the correction factor that was most discrepant from one. Asterisk indicates the preferred method of computing SEs for each model.

References

Abadie, Alberto, Susan Athey, Guido W. Imbens, and Jeffrey Wooldridge, "When Should You Adjust Standard Errors for Clustering?" Cambridge, Mass.: National Bureau of Economic Research, NBER Working Paper No. 24003, November 2017.

Akaike, Hirotugu, "A New Look at the Statistical Model Identification," *IEEE Transactions on Automatic Control*, Vol. 19, No. 6, December 1974, pp. 716–723.

Aneja, Abhay, John J. Donohue III, and Alexandria Zhang, "The Impact of Right-to-Carry Laws and the NRC Report: Lessons for the Empirical Evaluation of Law and Policy," *Stanford Law and Economics*, Olin Working Paper, No. 461, December 1, 2014. As of May 21, 2017:
https://papers.ssrn.com/sol3/papers.cfm?abstract_id=2443681

Angrist, Joshua D., and Jörn-Steffen Pischke, *Mostly Harmless Econometrics: An Empiricist's Companion*, Princeton, N.J.: Princeton University Press, 2009, pp. 227–243.

Arellano, M., "Computing Robust Standard Errors for Within-Group Estimators," *Oxford Bulletin of Economics and Statistics*, Vol. 49, No. 4, November 1987, pp. 431–434.

Barnett, Adrian G., Jolieke C. van Der Pols, and Annette J. Dobson, "Regression to the Mean: What It Is and How to Deal with It," *International Journal of Epidemiology*, Vol. 34, No. 1, February 2005, pp. 215–220.

Bertrand, Marianne, Esther Duflo, and Sendhil Mullainathan, "How Much Should We Trust Differences-in-Differences Estimates?" *Quarterly Journal of Economics*, Vol. 119, No. 1, February 1, 2004, pp. 249–275.

Bureau of Justice Statistics, "Corrections Statistical Analysis Tool (CSAT)—Prisoners," webpage, undated. As of July 20, 2018:
http://www.bjs.gov/index.cfm?ty=nps

Burnham, Kenneth P., and David R. Anderson, *Model Selection and Multimodel Inference: A Practical Information-Theoretic Approach*, 2nd ed., New York: Springer-Verlag, 2002.

Button, Katherine S., John P. A. Ioannidis, Claire Mokrysz, Brian A. Nosek, Jonathan Flint, Emma S. J. Robinson, and Marcus R. Munafò, "Power Failure: Why Small Sample Size Undermines the Reliability of Neuroscience," *Nature Reviews: Neuroscience*, Vol. 14, 2013, pp. 1–12.

CDC—*See* Centers for Disease Control and Prevention.

Centers for Disease Control and Prevention, "CDC WONDER," website, August 21, 2018. As of August 23, 2018:
https://wonder.cdc.gov/

Cheng, Cheng, and Mark Hoekstra, "Does Strengthening Self-Defense Law Deter Crime or Escalate Violence? Evidence from Expansions to Castle Doctrine," *Journal of Human Resources*, Vol. 48, No. 3, July 1, 2013, pp. 821–853.

Cochrane, Donald, and G. H. Orcutt, "Application of Least Squares Regression to Relationships Containing Auto-Correlated Error Terms," *Journal of the American Statistical Association*, Vol. 44, No. 245, January 1949, pp. 32–61

Cohen, Jacob, *Statistical Power Analysis for the Behavioral Sciences*, 2nd ed., Mahwah, N.J.: Lawrence Erlbaum Associates, 1988.

Crifasi, Cassandra K., John S. Meyers, Jon S. Vernick, and Daniel W. Webster, "Effects of Changes in Permit-to-Purchase Handgun Laws in Connecticut and Missouri on Suicide Rates," *Preventive Medicine*, Vol. 79, October 2015, pp. 43–49.

Cummings, Peter, David C. Grossman, Frederick P. Rivara, and Thomas D. Koepsell, "State Gun Safe Storage Laws and Child Mortality Due to Firearms," *JAMA,* Vol. 278, No. 13, 1997, pp. 1084–1086.

DeSimone, Jeffrey, Sara Markowitz, and Jing Xu, "Child Access Prevention Laws and Nonfatal Gun Injuries," *Southern Economic Journal*, Vol. 80, No. 1, July 2013, pp. 5–25.

District of Columbia v Heller, 554 U.S. 570, 2008.

Durlauf, Steven N., Salvador Navarro, and David A. Rivers, "Model Uncertainty and the Effect of Shall-Issue Right-to-Carry Laws on Crime," *European Economic Review*, Vol. 81, 2016, pp. 32–67.

Duwe, Grant, Tomislav Kovandzic, and Carlisle E. Moody, "The Impact of Right-to-Carry Concealed Firearm Laws on Mass Public Shootings," *Homicide Studies*, Vol. 6, No. 4, 2002, pp. 271–296.

Freedman, David A., "On the So-Called 'Huber Sandwich Estimator' and 'Robust Standard Errors,'" *American Statistician*, Vol. 60, No. 4, 2006, pp. 299–302.

Gelman, Andrew, and John Carlin, "Beyond Power Calculations: Assessing Type S (Sign) and Type M (Magnitude) Errors," *Perspectives on Psychological Science*, Vol. 9, No. 6, November 2014, pp. 641–651.

Gelman, Andrew, and Francis Tuerlinckx, "Type S Error Rates for Classical and Bayesian Single and Multiple Comparison Procedures," *Computational Statistics*, Vol. 15, No. 3, September 2000, pp. 373–390.

Gius, Mark, "An Examination of the Effects of Concealed Weapons Laws and Assault Weapons Bans on State-Level Murder Rates," *Applied Economics Letters*, Vol. 21, No. 4, 2014, pp. 265–267.

Gius, Mark, "The Effects of State and Federal Background Checks on State-Level Gun-Related Murder Rates," *Applied Economics*, Vol. 47, No. 38, 2015a, pp. 4090–4101.

Gius, Mark, "The Impact of Minimum Age and Child Access Prevention Laws on Firearm-Related Youth Suicides and Unintentional Deaths," *Social Science Journal*, Vol. 52, No. 2, 2015b, pp. 168–175.

Gius, Mark, "The Impact of State and Federal Assault Weapons Bans on Public Mass Shootings," *Applied Economics Letters*, Vol. 22, No. 4, 2015c, pp. 281–284.

Grambsch, Patricia, "Regression to the Mean, Murder Rates, and Shall-Issue Laws," *American Statistician*, Vol. 62, No. 4, 2008, pp. 289–295.

Greenland, Sander, James M. Robins, and Judea Pearl, "Confounding and Collapsibility in Causal Inference," *Statistical Science*, Vol. 14, No. 1, February 1999, pp. 29–46.

Hahn, Robert A., Oleg Bilukha, Alex Crosby, Mindy T. Fullilove, Akiva Liberman, Eve Moscicki, Susan Snyder, Farris Tuma, and Peter A. Briss, "Firearms Laws and the Reduction of Violence: A Systematic Review," *American Journal of Preventive Medicine*, Vol. 28, No. 2, Suppl. 2, February 2005, pp. 40–71.

Helland, Eric, and Alexander Tabarrok, "Using Placebo Laws to Test 'More Guns, Less Crime,'" *Advances in Economic Analysis and Policy*, Vol. 4, No. 1, 2004, pp. 1–9.

Hepburn, Lisa, Deborah Azrael, Matthew Miller, and David Hemenway, "The Effect of Child Access Prevention Laws on Unintentional Child Firearm Fatalities, 1979–2000," *Journal of Trauma-Injury Infection and Critical Care*, Vol. 61, No. 2, August 2006, pp. 423–428.

Hume, David, *An Enquiry Concerning Human Understanding*, Mineola, N.Y.: Dover Publications, Inc., [1748] 2004.

IPUMS CPS, "Current Population Survey Data for Social, Economic, and Health Research," undated. As of November 11, 2018: https://cps.ipums.org/cps/

Jöreskog, Karl G., "Estimation and Testing of Simplex Models," *British Journal of Mathematical and Stastistical Psychology*, Vol. 23, No. 2, November 1970, pp. 121–145.

Kalesan, Bindu, Matthew E. Mobily, Olivia Keiser, Jeffrey A. Fagan, and Sandro Galea, "Firearm Legislation and Firearm Mortaliy in the USA: A Cross-Sectional, State-Level Study," *Lancet*, Vol. 387, No. 10030, April 30, 2016, pp. 1847–1855.

Kendall, Todd D., and Robert Tamura, "Unmarried Fertility, Crime, and Social Stigma," *Journal of Law and Economics*, Vol. 53, No. 1, 2010, pp. 185–221.

Kish, Leslie, "Some Statistical Problems in Research Design," *American Sociological Review*, Vol. 24, No. 3, June 1959, pp. 328–338.

Kovandzic, Tomislav, Thomas B. Marvell, and Lynne M. Vieraitis, "The Impact of 'Shall-Issue' Concealed Handgun Laws on Violent Crime Rates—Evidence from Panel Data for Large Urban Cities," *Homicide Studies*, Vol. 9, No. 4, November 1, 2005, pp. 292–323.

La Valle, James M., "'Gun Control' vs. 'Self-Protection': A Case Against the Ideological Divide," *Justice Policy Journal*, Vol. 10, No. 1, Spring 2013, pp. 1–26.

La Valle, James M., and Thomas C. Glover, "Revisiting Licensed Handgun Carrying: Personal Protection or Interpersonal Liability?" *American Journal of Criminal Justice*, Vol. 37, No. 4, January 2012, pp. 580–601.

Lott, John R., Jr., *The Bias Against Guns: Why Almost Everything You've Heard About Gun Control Is Wrong*, Washington, D.C.: Regnery Publishing, Inc., 2003.

Lott, John R., Jr., *More Guns, Less Crime: Understanding Crime and Gun-Control Laws*, 3rd ed., Chicago, Ill.: University of Chicago Press, 2010.

Lott, John R., Jr., and D. B. Mustard, "Crime, Deterrence, and Right-to-Carry Concealed Handguns," *Journal of Legal Studies*, Vol. 26, No. 1, January 1997, pp. 1–68.

Ludwig, Jens, and Philip J. Cook, "Homicide and Suicide Rates Associated with Implementation of the Brady Handgun Violence Prevention Act," *JAMA*, Vol. 284, No. 5, August 2, 2000, pp. 585–591.

Martin, Robert A., and Richard L. Legault, "Systematic Measurement Error with State-Level Crime Data: Evidence from the 'More Guns, Less Crime' Debate," *Journal of Research in Crime and Delinquency*, Vol. 42, No. 2, May 2005, pp. 187–210.

Mill, John Stuart, *A System of Logic*, London: John W. Parker, West Strand, 1843.

Moody, Carlisle E., Thomas B. Marvell, Pau R. Zimmerman, and Fasil Alemante, "The Impact of Right-to-Carry Laws on Crime: An Exercise in Replication," *Review of Economics and Finance*, Vol. 4, 2014, pp. 33–43.

Morral, Andrew R., Terry Schell, and Margaret Tankard, *The Effectiveness of Gun Policies: The Magnitude and Sources of Disagreement Among Gun Policy Experts*, Santa Monica, Calif.: RAND Corporation, RR-2088/1-RC, 2018. As of July 20, 2018:
https://www.rand.org/pubs/research_reports/RR2088z1.html

National Institute on Alcohol Abuse and Alcoholism, "Surveillance Report #104," webpage, March 2016. As of July 20, 2018:
http://pubs.niaaa.nih.gov/publications/surveillance104/tab4-1_14.htm

National Research Council, *Firearms and Violence: A Critical Review*, Washington, D.C.: National Academies Press, 2004.

Pearl, Judea, *Causality: Models, Reasoning and Inference*, 2nd ed., New York: Cambridge University Press, 2009.

Raissian, Kerri M., "Hold Your Fire: Did the 1996 Federal Gun Control Act Expansion Reduce Domestic Homicides?" *Journal of Policy Analysis and Management*, Vol. 35, No. 1, Winter 2016, pp. 67–93.

RAND Corporation, "Gun Policy in America," webpage, undated. As of July 20, 2018:
https://www.rand.org/research/gun-policy.html

RAND Corporation, *The Science of Gun Policy: A Critical Synthesis of Research Evidence on the Effects of Gun Policies in the United States*, Santa Monica, Calif., RR-2088-RC, 2018. As of August 23, 2018:
https://www.rand.org/pubs/research_reports/RR2088.html

Roberts, Darryl W., "Intimate Partner Homicide: Relationships to Alcohol and Firearms," *Journal of Contemporary Criminal Justice*, Vol. 25, No. 1, 2009, pp. 67–88.

Robins, James M., Miguel Ángel Hernan, and Babette Brumback, "Marginal Structural Models and Causal Inference in Epidemiology," Vol. 11, No. 5, September 2000, pp. 550–560.

Rosengart, M., P. Cummings, A. Nathens, P. Heagerty, R. Maier, and F. Rivara, "An Evaluation of State Firearm Regulations and Homicide and Suicide Death Rates," *Injury Prevention*, Vol. 11, No. 2, 2005, pp. 77–83.

Rubin, Donald B., "Assignment to Treatment Group on the Basis of a Covariate," *Journal of Educational Statistics*, Vol. 2, No. 1, Spring 1977, pp. 1–26.

Sen, Bisakha, and Anantachai Panjamapirom, "State Background Checks for Gun Purchase and Firearm Deaths: An Exploratory Study," *Preventive Medicine*, Vol. 55, No. 4, October 2012, pp. 346–350.

Siegel, Michael, Ziming Xuan, Craig S. Ross, Sandro Galea, Bindu Kalesan, Eric Fleegler, and Kristin A. Goss, "Easiness of Legal Access to Concealed Firearm Permits and Homicide Rates in the United States," *American Journal of Public Health*, Vol. 107, No. 12, December 1, 2017, pp. 1923–1929.

Simmons, Joseph P., Leif D. Nelson, and Uri Simonsohn, "False-Positive Psychology," *Psychological Science*, Vol. 22, No. 11, 2011, pp. 1359–1366.

Standish, William R., Thomas D. Cook, and Donald T. Campbell, *Experimental and Quasi-Experimental Designs for Generalized Causal Inference*, 2nd ed., Boston, Mass., and New York: Houghton Mifflin Company, 2002.

U.S. Census Bureau, "Population and Housing Unit Estimates," undated. As of November 12, 2018:
https://www.census.gov/programs-surveys/popest/data/data-sets.html

U.S. Census Bureau, "Historical Poverty Tables: People and Families—1959 to 2017," August 28, 2018. As of November 12, 2018:
https://www.census.gov/data/tables/time-series/demo/income-poverty/historical-poverty-people.html

U.S. Department of Justice, Federal Bureau of Investigation, "2016 Law Enforcement Officers Killed and Assaulted," 2016. As of November 12, 2018:
https://ucr.fbi.gov/leoka/2016

U.S. Department of Labor, Bureau of Labor Statistics, "Local Area Unemployment Statistics," undated. As of November 11, 2018:
https://www.bls.gov/lau/data.htm

U.S. Department of Transportation, National Highway Traffic Safety Administration, *Lives Saved FAQs*, Washington, D.C., DOT HS 811 105, December 2009. As of July 20, 2018:
https://crashstats.nhtsa.dot.gov/Api/Public/ViewPublication/811105

U.S. Fish and Wildlife Service, Wildlife and Sport Fish Restoration Program, "Historical Hunting License Data," September 12, 2018. As of November 12, 2018:
https://wsfrprograms.fws.gov/subpages/licenseinfo/hunting.htm

VanderWeele, Tyler J., and Ilya Shpitser, "A New Criterion for Confounder Selection," *Biometrics*, Vol. 67, No. 4, December 2011, pp. 1406–1413.

Vigdor, Elizabeth R., and James A. Mercy, "Do Laws Restricting Access to Firearms by Domestic Violence Offenders Prevent Intimate Partner Homicide?" *Evaluation Review*, Vol. 30, No. 3, 2006, pp. 313–346.

Webster, Daniel, Cassandra Kercher Crifasi, and Jon S. Vernick, "Effects of the Repeal of Missouri's Handgun Purchaser Licensing Law on Homicides," *Journal of Urban Health*, Vol. 91, No. 2, April 2014, pp. 293–302.

Webster, Daniel W., and Marc Starnes, "Reexamining the Association Between Child Access Prevention Gun Laws and Unintentional Shooting Deaths of Children," *Pediatrics*, Vol. 106, No. 6, December 2000, pp. 1466–1469.

Webster, Daniel W., Jon S. Vernick, April M. Zeoli, and Jennifer A. Manganello, "Association Between Youth-Focused Firearm Laws and Youth Suicides," *Journal of the American Medical Association*, Vol. 292, No. 5, August 2004, pp. 594–601.

White, Halbert, "A Heteroskedasticity-Consistent Covariance Matrix and a Direct Test for Heteroskedasticity," *Econometrica*, Vol. 48, No. 4, May 1980, pp. 817–838.

Wooldridge, Jeffrey M., *Econometric Analysis of Cross Section and Panel Data*, 2nd ed., Cambridge, Mass.: MIT Press, 2010.

Yuan, Ke-Hai, and Peter M. Bentler, "Three Likelihood-Based Methods for Mean and Covariance Structure Analysis with Nonnormal Missing Data," *Sociological Methodology*, Vol. 30, No. 1, 2000, pp. 165–200.

Zeileis, Achim, "Econometric Computing with HC and HAC Covariance Matrix Estimators," *Journal of Statistical Software*," Vol. 11, No. 10, 2004, pp. 1–17.

Zeileis, Achim, "Object-Oriented Computation of Sandwich Estimators," *Journal of Statistical Software*, Vol. 16, No. 9, 2006, pp. 1–16.

Zeoli, April M., and Daniel W. Webster, "Effects of Domestic Violence Policies, Alcohol Taxes and Police Staffing Levels on Intimate Partner Homicide in Large U.S. Cities," *Injury Prevention*, Vol. 16, No. 2, 2010, pp. 90–95.

About the Authors

Terry L. Schell is a senior behavioral scientist at the RAND Corporation. His research has focused on posttraumatic stress disorder among civilian survivors of community violence and service members who served in Iraq and Afghanistan. Schell has conducted research on sexual assault in the U.S. military, the long-term effects of violence on mental health, the effectiveness of criminal rehabilitation programs, racial equity in policing, and the effects of gun policies on firearm deaths, among other topics.

Beth Ann Griffin is a senior statistician at the RAND Corporation, where she codirects the RAND Center for Causal Inference and is a professor at the Pardee RAND Graduate School. Her statistical research focuses on causal effects estimation when using observational data. She is the principal investigator of two projects sponsored by the National Institute of Drug Abuse and serves on the editorial board of the *Annals of Applied Statistics, Statistics in Medicine and Observational Studies.*

Andrew R. Morral is a senior behavioral scientist at the RAND Corporation, where he leads its Gun Policy in America initiative. His research areas include program evaluation, modeling and simulation, survey research, and performance measurement. Recent work includes an evaluation of the prevalence and characteristics of sexual assault in the U.S. military, an evaluation of the Israel Police, and two studies of the deterrence benefits attributable to counterterrorism security systems.

Made in the USA
Monee, IL
21 September 2022

14393587R00066